Global Responsible Intergenerational Leadership

A conceptual framework and implementation guidance for intergenerational fairness

Julia M. Puaschunder
Columbia University

Vernon Series in Economics

VERNON PRESS

www.vernonpress.com

In the Americas:
Vernon Press
1000 N West Street,
Suite 1200, Wilmington,
Delaware 19801
United States

In the rest of the world:
Vernon Press
C/Sancti Espiritu 17,
Malaga, 29006
Spain

Vernon Series in Economics

Library of Congress Control Number: 2017948824

ISBN: 978-1-62273-241-8

Cover design by Vernon Press, using elements selected by freepik.

Julia M. Puaschunder*

The New School, Department of Economics, Schwartz Center for Economic Policy Analysis,

6 East 16th Street, 11th floor 1129F-99, New York, NY 10003, USA, Julia.Puaschunder@newschool.edu, T 001 21222957004905, M 001 7188778871,

F 001 2122295724, http://juliampuaschunder.com/

Columbia University, Graduate School of Arts and Sciences, 116th Street Broadway, New York, New York 10027, USA, Julia.Puaschunder@columbia.edu, http://blogs.cuit.columbia.edu/jmp2265/

* Financial support of the Association for Social Economics, Austrian Academy of Science, Austrian Federal Ministry of Science, Austrian Office of Science and Technology at the Austrian Embassy to the United States of America, Bard Center for Environmental Policy, Research and Economy, Elisabeth und Helmut Uhl Stiftung, Eugene Lang Liberal Arts College of The New School, International Association for Political Science Students, Finance, Risk and Accounting Perspectives Conference at University of Cambridge, Fritz Thyssen Foundation, Federal Ministry of Education and Research of the Federal Republic of Germany (Bundesministerium für Bildung und Forschung der Bundesrepublik Deutschland), George Washington University, Georgia State University Center for the Economic Analysis of Risk, HSBC Bank USA, Huebner Foundation for Insurance Education, INSEAD Initiative for Learning Innovation and Teaching Excellence, Harvard University Center for the Environment, ideas42, International Institute for Applied Systems Analysis, Janeway Center Fellowship, Max Kade Foundation New York, the New School for Social Research, New York (Dean's List, Endowment Stipend, Fee Board Scholarship, President's Scholarship), New School University Senate, Oxford Academic Research Network, Prize Fellowship in the Inter-University Consortium of New York, Tishman Environment and Design Center, University of Kent, University of Vienna, Science and Technology Global Consortium, Vernon Art and Science and the Vienna University of Economics and Business is gratefully acknowledged. The author declares no conflict of interest. All omissions, errors and misunderstandings in this piece are solely the author's.

To future generations

Exposé

Globalization leveraged pressure on contemporary society. Today's most pressing social dilemmas regarding climate change, overindebtedness, and aging Western world populations demand to rethink capitalism. Understanding the bounds of capitalism to avoid ethical downfalls beyond the control of singular nation states infringing on intergenerational equity – the fairness to provide an at least as favorable standard of living to future generations as enjoyed today – has become a blatant demand. In a history of turning to natural law as a human-imbued moral compass for solving societal downfalls on a global scale in times of crises; this book captures the natural human drive towards intergenerational fairness in order to retrieve information on how to implement intergenerational justice. Based on the idea of intergenerational equity as a natural behavioral law, the monograph theoretically outlines the current societal demand for eternal equity and proposes intergenerational justice theories. Intertemporal connectedness and interaction of overlapping generations enable intergenerational benefits transfers and burden sharing, which will be discussed. Social mobility within networks comprised of different generations is enhanced through social upward movement opportunities. In addition, meritocracy helps alleviate intergenerational inequality. Vanishing social status prospects, a concurrent presentation of intertemporal perspectives but also trust and reciprocity drive intergenerational responsibility. Overall, portraying intergenerational conscientiousness as humane-imbued cue strengthens the legal case for integrating intergenerational fairness in policy frameworks on a global basis. In addition, describing intergenerational care as something natural that has been practiced ever since, will spearhead interdisciplinary endeavors to solve contemporary predicaments between overlapping generations. Exploring intergenerational opportunities is targeted at innovatively guiding the implementation of justice over time and between generations. Strengthening financial social responsibility, social welfare, and environmental protection through future-oriented and socially responsible economic market approaches in the 21st century is aimed at alleviating predictable economic, social and environmental crises to ensure a future sustainable humankind for this generation and the following.

Table of Contents

Chapter 1

Introduction

We live in interesting times. From the sixteenth century age of enlightenment, science and technology remarkably revolutionized the world. Followed by the eighteenth-century industrialization, technological advancements, technical inventions, and capital accumulation leveraged the standard of living for humankind. The post-WWII economic boom heralded golden years of socio-economic advancement and economic capital growth outpacing every measure previous ages had known.

Though looking back to an epoch of enormous economic progress in the 20th century; the improvement of living conditions seemed to be slowed from the turn of the millennium on due to the impact of unforeseeable system fragility. The era of globalization, featuring complex interconnections and transactions faster than ever before in history, appeared to imply emergent systemic risks (Centeno & Tham, 2012). What happens in one part of the world today impacts around the globe. The global interconnectedness imposing dangers creates a need for framework conditions securing from negative consequences emerging from the new web of social, ecological and fundamental transfers on a grand scale (Centeno, Cinlar, Cloud, Creager, DiMaggio, Dixit, Elga, Felten, James, Katz, Keohane, Leonard, Massey, Mian, Mian, Oppenheimer, Shafir & Shapiro, 2013).

Tomorrow's children may not enjoy the same standard of living as Western world economies in the eye of climate change, overindebtedness and heightened austerity demands but also in light of aging demography problems. Global challenges of climate change but also overindebtedness in the aftermath of the 2008/09 World Financial Crisis currently raise attention to transnational intertemporal fairness. Intergenerational equity nowadays has come into public scrutiny entering the academic and practical discourse in the public and private sectors.

Since the 2008/09 World Financial Crisis pervaded societal demand to increase the socio-ethical commitments of corporations. Social awareness due to mass media reporting heightened stakeholder pressure exerting influence on corporate decision makers for ethicality. Therefore today's most pressing societal long-term downfalls call for corporate social activities to back governmental regulation to steer intergenerational justice.

In the implementation of intergenerational equity, the age of globalization shifted the influence of national governments and their policies as a predominant force in the economy to international governance of the corporate sector. Since decisions in one country can directly affect the interest of citizens of other societies in a completely new range of trans-boundary problems, the influence and efficacy of national democracy are challenged. Limits to and the constraints on national economic autonomy and sovereignty have become blatant due to increased international interdependence. With political uncertainty in light of fluctuations between free trade and protectionism poles, corporatism should step in on societal downfalls (Panitch & Gindin, 2012). Holding widespread access to vital economic resources and markets, today multinationals have become quasi-global governance institutions that leveraged into implicit legal and political authorities to regulate economic activity in the architecture of the world economy.

External shocks of economic depressions and wars of the past affected the quality of life of the young ever since and steered attention to social responsibility (Puaschunder, 2015c). But what future risks and opportunities arise for future perspectives of the youth today in the aftermath of the 2008/09 World Financial Crisis given unprecedented governmental overindebtedness, an aging Western world population and the irreversible environmental damages is unknown. Intergenerational equity research has thus unprecedented momentum.

In the eye of a current pressing demand for attention to intergenerational equity in the domains of climate justice and austerity, the following book theoretically highlights the corporate world's potential to alleviate current intergenerational equity imbalances and explores intergenerational justice implementation strategies of the corporate world and the public sector.

The following book is targeted at promoting the idea of intergenerational equity and intertemporal harmoniously balanced transfers in the public and corporate world as an alternative to national governance and a novel extension of contemporary Corporate Social Responsibility (CSR) models. Intergenerational responsible leadership is built on the idea that corporate executives have an obligation to incorporate needs of far-ranging constituents, including future generations.

This monograph is designed to help readers understand intergenerational equity leadership from different angles. It is aimed at helping people who are motivated to learn about contemporary intergenerational equity constraints in the domains of finance, economics, and ecologic sustainability. A broad readership comprising of leaders from academia, the legislative branch and public policy-making, who consider implementing intergenerational balance, should be engaged. Intergenerational equity implementation recommendations are given to serve academics, public executives and private sector representatives.

Investigating intergenerational equity is a formidable task as for touching on unprecedented predicaments comprising manifold stakeholders. An engagement of various stakeholders on the differing intergenerational predicaments results in a disparity of intergenerational equity notions. As a first step towards resolving societal losses imbued in the complexity of this novel phenomenon but also to innovatively explore new opportunities to ingrain intergenerational responsibility within globalizing economies; the following research will study intergenerational equity with special attention to expert opinions and stakeholder facets in the interplay of public and private sector approaches. Holistically describing intergenerational equity with attention to stakeholders' perspectives helps overcome socio-economic losses implied by various societal notions. Averting multi-stakeholder conflicts in the implementation of intergenerational equity will aid harmonizing intergenerational equity on a grand scale.

When investigating the natural human intergenerational conscientiousness, behavioral economics insights on human decision-making are innovatively considered. Behavioral economics depict human rationality bounded by mental limitations and heuristic decision shortcuts in an overly complex governmental architecture over which political leaders have limited control (Tversky & Kahneman, 1974). These errors are crucial in ethical considerations with an irreversible impact on society. The emerging field of bounded ethicality describes predictable psychological processes that let people engage in ethically questionable behavior inconsistent with their preferred ethics. Bounded ethicality occurs when ethical individuals are unaware of indirect unethical consequences that erode over time (Bazerman & Chugh, 2005; Bazerman & Moore, 2008; Tenbrunsel & Messick, 2004). While bounded ethicality research offers a way to capture intergenerational conscientiousness realistically, we miss a whole-rounded intergenerational equity decision-making frame to test the applicability of the bounded ethicality paradigm onto intergenerational concerns and explore motives for sacrificing to future generations within the social compound.

Intergenerational conscientiousness requires social responsibility and intertemporal foresight to discount future lives. In the search to alleviate human bounded ethicality on intertemporal dilemmas, emotions were recently found to influence time perspectives and social responsibility (Horberg, Oveis & Keltner, 2011). Emotionally laden intergenerational values appear as windows of opportunity to steer intergenerational ethicality in human decision-making. Trust – as a concept related to emotionality – could be an additional intergenerational ethicality nudging to overcome the lack of identification with future beneficiaries (Ostrom, 2009).

Based on a theoretical introduction of intergenerational equity as a natural behavioral law in this book (Puaschunder, 2015c), expert knowledge will therefore theoretically fortify the idea of intergenerational equity as a natural behavioral law. Retrieving a framework of intergenerational equity challenges regarding an aging population, overindebtedness and ecological constraints with attention to stakeholder-specific public and private sector approaches and depicting potential human intergenerational conscientiousness bounds and triggers will allow deriving recommendations for well-balanced intergenerational equity public and private sector implementation solutions.

Based on exploratory expert information on intergenerational equity, the social representations on intergenerational equity reveal stakeholder-specificities of intergenerational responsibility in order to compare intergenerational equity practices and trends throughout the global arena. Addressing stakeholder-specificities of intergenerational responsibility will holistically capture intergenerational equity in the post-2008/09 World Financial Crisis era. A more sophisticated investigation of stakeholder-nuanced intergenerational responsibility will pay attention to public and private sector intergenerational contributions.

Outlining intergenerational equity implementation solutions helps individuals and politicians to make decisions with respect for future generations and establish socially responsible leadership. New ways how to change lifestyles that lead to sustainable and intergenerationally conscientious living are suggested featuring insights on societal decision-making and collective choices. Intergenerational conscientiousness nudges are retrieved in the literature and tested in field and laboratory experiments. The relation of emotions, trust and social forces regarding common goods allocation preferences is outlined in order to enhance intergenerational, social conscientiousness.

Individual decision-making on intergenerational equity is coupled with studies on multivariate and network analyses of public and private intergenerational equity considerations throughout the global arena.

Featuring differing constituencies, international consensus finding on intergenerational equity is hindered as parts of the world are more affected than others. While intergenerational equity is a global problem, there are vast national differences in its manifestation and implementation. In the opening, booming economies – foremost China, India and other Asian novel power nations – the upcoming generation has enormous advantages compared to the past. In free market economies, an upcoming population with no siblings to share enjoys unprecedented access to wealth and opportunities. The Asian youth have been on the receiving end of enormous wealth accumulated in a very short time. The solutions to current Western world intergenerational problems are connected to the rise of these nations and Western pension funds may be pegged to emerging markets. Problematic appears that growing economies with increasing population will have a higher resource consumption and energy demand putting sustainable consumption endeavors at stake.

Arising ethical questions if these emerging cultures have the same right as the Western world had centuries ago – in the age of industrialization – to consume and prosper in the eye of climate change will be posed.

International comparisons of intergenerational social welfare schemes will drive public and private sector recommendations on intergenerational equity contributions in the interplay of favorable market incentive structures and prescriptive public policies. Investigating intergenerational equity before and after the 2008/09 World Financial Crisis will fortify our understanding of intergenerational equity as a risk management and crisis prevention strategy. The unprecedented impact of an aging Western world population on social welfare service provision with special attention to Eurozone frictions arising from the combination of bailouts and an aging, shrinking Euro-population will be outlined.

Theoretically describing and empirically testing human intergenerational ethicality introduces intergenerational equity as a natural behavioral law. In a history of turning to natural law for solving societal predicaments on a global scale in times of crises; understanding intergenerational equity as a natural behavioral law alleviates potential aggression potential between generations and promotes a sustainable humankind. Capturing intergenerational equity as a natural behavioral law backs the legal case for sustainability, stimulates the academic discourse and allows aligning diverse stakeholder notions on intergenerational concerns. Acknowledging intergenerational equity as a natural behavioral law establishes the legal basis for global justice in order to leverage eternal equity into universal and impartial human rights over time. Applying bounded ethicality onto financial and environmental considerations interdisciplinarily spearheads behavioral law and economics models and fosters an accurate understanding of the limitations of human social responsibility on intergenerational conscientiousness. Both approaches, capturing intergenerational equity theoretically and empirically, help averting intergenerational tensions and work towards intergenerational balance in-between generations.

Drawing a picture of the shared common sense on intergenerational equity, but also revealing stakeholder-specific nuances helps diminish communication barriers and aligns less coherent viewpoints on intergenerational fairness. Contributing to new socio-economic thinking on intergenerational equity aids our understanding of the social representations of intergenerational equity as an opportunity to forecast individual behavior as well as predict future intergenerational trends. Capturing stakeholder-specific expert knowledge allows deriving recommendations to lead academics, technocrats, and practitioners to reflect deeper on intergenerational conscientiousness. Stakeholder-specific facets of intergenerational responsibility advance our knowledge on the well-tempered interplay of responsible market actors and governmental oversight control as vital ingredients of *Generationspartnerships.* Gaining first-hand insights from public and private factors on intergenerational equity allows to predicting on how to build public-private-partnerships in order to alleviate intergenerational frictions. Knowledge of stakeholder-specific success factors also reduces socio-economic losses imbued in the complexity of the novel phenomenon and aids a harmonious implementation of intergenerational responsibility.

Empirically finding human-imbued, future-oriented intergenerational ethicality provides evidence for the legal codification of intergenerational fairness on an international basis. Expert knowledge coupled with behavioral economic insights on how to improve human cognition regarding future-orientation and social responsibility aids the administration of intergenerational equity. Deriving information on circumstances under which decision makers are likely to be intergenerationally conscientious is targeted at outlining ways how to additionally improve intergenerational equity in the absence of law enforcement and governmental control. Finding responsibility triggers helps designing contexts that advance intergenerational equity to complement institutional policies. Unraveling intergenerational equity downfall risks enables institutional technocrats to better design contexts that automatically raise future orientation and open ways to steer civic duty compliance based on a cooperative government-citizen relationship regarding intergenerational concerns.

Investigating intergenerational constraints from a global governance perspective helps understanding the impact of public and private sector contributions on intergenerational fairness. Studying public welfare problems as well as financial market predicaments and environmental constraints concurrently elucidate similarities and differences between public and private sector approaches to ensure intergenerational equity. Mapping intergenerational equity throughout the world allows international comparisons of public and private sector intergenerational responsibility endeavors in order to derive multi-faceted success factors for a concerted implementation of intergenerational responsibility. Paying attention to the 2008/09 World Financial Crisis provides a unique snapshot of socio-economic changes implied by a financial turmoil and helps portraying crises as an opportunity for ingraining ethicality throughout society. In sum, understanding the socio-dynamics of intergenerational equity will serve as a prerequisite for an intergenerationally harmonious and a future sustainable humanity.

Chapter 2

Eternal Equity in the Fin-de-Millenaire

Tomorrow's children may not have the same standard of living as aging Western world populations may experience economies struck by high unemployment coupled with governmental overindebtedness in the aftermath of the 2008/09 world financial crisis. As a consequence of complex economic interconnections, market prosperity burst with the 2008/09 monetary downturn having evolved from individual ethical failures amalgamating into collective downfalls (Streeck, 2011). We now not only suffer from the painful readjustment between economic fluctuations and whimsical market movements in the finance world. Market failures also having been compensated by the public results in an unprecedented overindebtedness of the Western world. Budget crises around the world led to austerity plans triggering an economic climate of stagnation, federal spending constraints and prospected social welfare decline for decades to come (Ghilarducci & McGahey, 2013).

In the aftermath of the 2008/09 World Financial Crisis, the finance sector is under scrutiny as for having made fast capital at the expense of the real economy. Since 2009 financial institutions are publicly pressured to justify their social impacts and responsibility. Economic pessimism grows in the belief that the current equity imbalances will be long term and cause the next generation being worse off. The destruction of assets and degrading of capital values led to a devaluation of personal property. What followed was the unorganized uprising in the wake of an uncontrolled clash of realities. Distributive equity claims and the call for equality of opportunities rose in economically troubled areas. Direct democracy protests culminated in the Occupy Wall Street movement. People having lost trust in banking systems, started to think about future obligations and more than ever before now strive to pass on an as favorable standard of living for future generations.

In the eye of our children having to pay for our current economic recovery, we are now taking from future generations. Not only do we live at their expenses, but the youth also not quite has the same opportunities as their parents enjoyed. Rising prices take away wealth accumulation prospects and austerity plans diminish access to social welfare. Missing budgetary resources result in governmental education cuts. The societal outcomes are crucial to the people who experience hope for a better future through educational opportunities. Restricted access to education breeds social immobility. 'Born poor, die poor' becomes a reality in the Western world and an intergenerational equity constraint, when European students have to pay for their tuition while generations before were granted free access to knowledge.

In addition, employment opportunities for this generation are more limited than for prior generations. Within Europe, in 2012 the overall European Union (EU) unemployment rate stood at 11.4% but featured a distorted pattern. Based on the EU accession of 2004, old 'core' member states (EU 15) and EU-2004 accession 'periphery' member states (EU12) differ on employment significantly. When comparing core with peripheral countries, we find in the core a relatively lower mean unemployment rate of 7.54%[1] compared to 15.04% mean unemployment in the periphery[2] (Puaschunder, 2016b).

Unemployment hits the European youth the hardest. In many parts of the Western world, it has become almost impossible to get a job for the young – for instance, in 2011 the Spanish youth faced an up to 65% high unemployment rate. As of January 2013, Spain's unemployment rate was 26.2%, and for those under 25 years, the rate remained around 60% (Eurostat, 2015). Greece featured an overall unemployment rate of 27% and 59% for individuals under 25 years. Of the under the age of 25 years workforce, 23.7% were unemployed in the Eurozone and 21.9% in the overall EU as of November 2014. The youth in the core EU faces a mean unemployment rate of 18.3%,[3] while the periphery youth stands at 29.1%[4] as of November 2014. Long-term unemployment is highest in the Slovak Republic, Germany (with former East Germany accounting for high unemployment, as ever since the reunification in 1990, the unemployment rate in the East has been almost twice that of the West), Poland and Greece.

There is also an explosion of unpaid internships that further breed social inequality as the market turns the workforce to having to afford to work.

---

[1] based on Austria 4.9%, Belgium 8.8%, Czech Republic 7.1%, Denmark 6%, Finland 8.1%, France 10.2%, Germany 5.3%, Hungary 8.1%, Italy 13%, Luxembourg 4.9%, Malta 6.4%, Netherlands 8.3%, Sweden 8.1%, and UK 6.3% as of 2013 and 2014.

[2] based on Bulgaria 11.6%, Croatia 21.6%, Cyprus 17.4%, Estonia 10.9%, Greece 27.9%, Ireland 10.7%, Latvia 9.8%, Lithuania 12.4%, Poland 10.3%, Portugal 16.8%, Romania 7.3%, Slovakia 14.4%, Slovenia 13.1%, Spain 26.3% as of 2013.

[3] based on core countries Austria 8.9%, Belgium 21.6%, Czech Republic 15.6%, Denmark 11.4%, Finland 20.7%, France 25.4%, Germany 7.4%, Hungary 19.8%, Italy 43.9%, Luxembourg 18.4%, Malta 13.5%, Netherlands 9.7%, Sweden 23%, and UK 16.3%.

[4] periphery countries Bulgaria 21.4%, Croatia 45.5%, Cyprus 34.8%, Estonia 13.9%, Greece 49.8%, Ireland 21.8%, Latvia 20.3%, Lithuania 15.5%, Poland 23.2%, Portugal 34.5%, Romania 23.3%, Slovakia 29.2%, Slovenia 20.4%, and Spain 53.5% national unemployment rates.

Countries with current high unemployment like Spain, Italy, and Ireland, in which the youth turns to black market labor, leave the government with lower tax revenues and the young without perspectives and trust in their government. Unemployment not only opens generation gaps. Negative socio-psychological consequences arise out of fear of the future, which may become a self-fulfilling proficiency of economic depression.

Young people see their prospects vanishing and are left without hope for a better future when they experience their decision-making not being included in the political will. The young struggle with the anonymity of governmental support and their experienced helplessness drives anger. Starting in the fall of 2009 in Vienna, the 'Uni brennt' ('University is burning') student occupation of the University of Vienna's Audimax advocated for social equality, access to education and minority empowerment. The protests lasted for months and inflamed uproar all over Europe. In the face of social responsibility declines, protests fueled to release societal tensions. Spain's youth suffering from over 65% unemployment and fading future perspectives rebelled during the summer of 2011, which spread all across Europe supported by new media tools – like blogs, Facebook, and Twitter. The popular media has been puzzled in describing a uniting theme of the contemporary populace on the street. With the young going on the streets for protests in the Western world, unprecedented intergenerational imbalances, one may argue, are driving this trend.

Exhausted twin deficits of current and capital account put extraordinary burdens on the upcoming generation. An American child, for instance, is born into 59,000 USD debt per capita and a US taxpayer owes more 160,000 USD share of governmental debt with trends predicting a grim outlook. In the end, the children of tomorrow will not only pay the price for our currently taken up debt. Placing the holders' current pension consumption payment obligations onto the young is problematic, as pensions are usually not allocated towards future investments – such as infrastructure or education, which would build future societal assets in the long run and make future generations richer. The debt burden gains weight when considering the societal trend of a shrinking Western world population. As the problem appears as a long-term crisis, unemployment will rise, individual prosperity decline and social welfare standards degrade.

The standard of living we have today will have to be maintained by a demographically shrinking body of young, who will have to uphold the current way of life. In the aging Western population, we see the workforce shifting to pensioners. Western, and in particular European pension systems, become unfeasible with current debt accumulation to pay out pensions, which breed inequality in European low-inheritance tax countries. Rising social security expenditures due to medical advancements and pension payments growing with an enlarging body of retired already cause frictions in the social compound. A pension system reform is insofar complicated, as the age pyramid has already tipped in most European countries featuring more receivers in the voting booth than payers. In addition, in a loss-avert world, cutting given promises equals political suicide. The European fiscal union requiring transnational financial bailouts will breed inequality in legally differing tax and pension territories. 58% of social protection spending is based in Europe. For instance, why should a 55-year old early pensioner in one country receive tax subsidies enabled by a 65-year employee in another region of the EU?

While monetary values can be rebuilt, capitalism's myopic *short-term* profit systematically ignores the broader and longer-ranging implications of its actions and externalities, which results in irreversible ecological destruction (Boscov-Ellen, 2015).

Contemporary capitalism raises ecological limits to growth and environment concerns in the eye of unsustainable resource consumption and increasing man-made climate change (Zaretsky, 2015). Regarding climate change and ecologic sustainability, the world appears more vulnerable than ever before. In 2010 we hit the highest energy resource consumption in the 40-year recording of sustainability. Climate change is going to be the greatest human challenge of the 21st century touching on all human rights given the potential massive and widespread impacts creating irreversible lock-ins for future generations and injustice over time. The destruction of the environment is the most sustainable peril of globalization.

Overall, not only an aging Western world population and the 2008/09 World Financial Crisis but also climate change pressure our children to come. In a climate of economic downturn and growing burden to support the elderly, our children will also face declining biodiversity and ecological, environmental changes in the wake of climate change. Figure 1 holds the currently most pressing intergenerational equity constraints of the Western world.

Figure 1: Intergenerational equity constraints

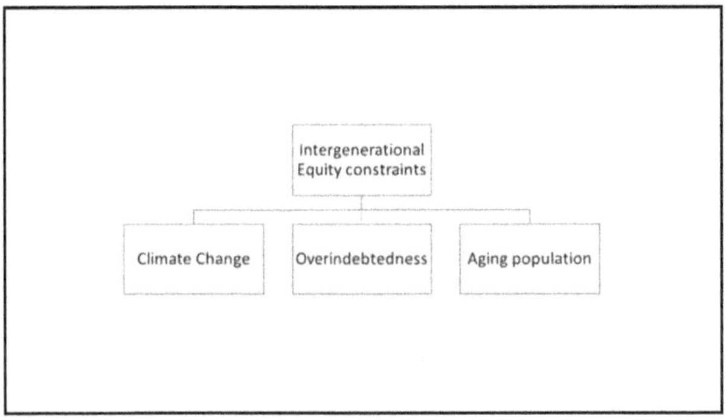

This unprecedented intergenerational kink in the domains of climate stability, overindebtedness, and social welfare reform needs heralds an overall call for intergenerational equity – the fairness to provide an at least as favorable standard of living as enjoyed today. As we realize that our children may not have the same chances as we do, we must strive for global equity over time. The global challenge is thereby to find sustainable, qualitative economic growth in harmony with human rights of development over time.

The idea of eternal equity addresses justice over time. As an implicit contract and transfer between living and future generations, intergenerational equity not only reduces unfairness for future world inhabitants who are born in less favorable environmental conditions than their parents. Intergenerational equity also ensures future infrastructure, equal opportunities over time and constant access to social welfare for the youth. Intergenerational equity grants a favorable climate between generations and averts frictions arising from austerity plans, diminishing social welfare standards and declining environmental prosperity. Intergenerational equity avoids discriminating against future generations on the basis of the remoteness of the time at which they will live.

While intergenerational equity is as old as humankind – the 2008/09 World Financial Crisis, an aging industrialized world and climate change have put a new stance on the dimensions of overindebtedness and irreversible destruction of future potential, which may serve as an explanation for the 2011 occupy Zeitgeist reclaiming public space as a symbol for common goods (Fraser, 2014; Nafeez, 2013). In the eye of leaving next generations' debt, unfeasible social welfare and sustainability threats, intergenerational equity is an urgent topic of concern that opens windows of opportunity to implement financial, social responsibility, social pension reform and ecologic sustainability (Magdoff & Foster, 2010).

The complex challenges ahead will require heightened attention to future generations' well-being. In the eye of an unprecedented intergenerational equity kink, it has become economically efficient to think about the next generation and future world-inhabitants' living conditions. The prevailing world depression, the enormous anomaly of unemployment and liquidity constraints not only make instant economic market stimulus necessary but also the demographic shifts demand foresighted governance.

While the wish for intergenerational equity has sparked, we currently lack a codified legal framework on intergenerational fairness as well as an economic understanding of feasible intergenerational equity models that accurately pay attention to future generations. To measure intergenerational equity, we will have to estimate future developments. Intergenerational equity will require discounting of future events by politicians, policy makers and private individuals who will have to factor in future-orientation and social responsibility in current decisions. Future world inhabitants must be put into the focus of today's choices by shifting the current wealth of the elderly to save for future generations and put sustainable governance in place. We may also have to curb our consumption rates or find alternative climate justice financing strategies to conscientiously transmit the earth's resources to future generations (Puaschunder, 2016a).

The outlined intergenerational equity constraints are complex and their solution interdependent. As the present crisis has exposed the weaknesses of orthodox economic theory, novel heterodox economic thinking is demanded (Shaikh, 2013). The current world economy opens possibilities but also threatens future generations. While economic growth may aid a soft landing with current liquidity constraints, booming markets also imply heightened energy consumption trading-off from the ecologic quality of life in the long run. Entrepreneurial solutions may ease the overindebtedness, but innovation in the medical sector will explode medical care expenditures for pensioners – especially in social welfare territories obeying to mandatorily provide the best medical aid available to their citizens. Governments must breed hope through forward-looking strategies in the eye of radical austerity cuts and unemployment gaps to take away people's fear of the future. Policy makers are pressured to revise social services and rise the retirement age in industrialized economies. Intergenerational equity constraints may not be solved through governmental programs alone but coupled with ever since existing intergenerational conscientiousness expression in communities.

Eternal equity has always been lived within the family compound and practiced in the wake of humane fairness notions. The human-imbued wish to provide an at least as favorable standard of living to our children stems from evolutionary, social and religious values. Ignorance regarding intergenerational concerns naturally feels wrong, and the hegemony of the 'now' appears like a sin on future generations. Not being intergenerationally conscientious puts offspring at stake and detaches people from their environment. Understanding intergenerational conscientiousness as a natural behavioral humane-imbued law will help integrating future conditions in today's decision-making (Luf, 2011).

Building on Rawls' (1971) procedural justice, intergenerational equity will ensure fairness between generations based on future orientation and social responsibility for future generations. Pursuing intergenerational equity in the wish to provide a decent standard of living for the upcoming young can be enabled by a mutual transfer between old and young. Justice can be sought in future outlooks, humane reflexivity and globalized solidarity enabling that one generation does not overconsume at the expense of future generations.

Financial Social Responsibility will ensure that the current generation is not spending the money of tomorrow's children or takes up debt to be paid by future children. Generations passing on assets to the future will feature age-attentively redistributed wealth, investments for young and respect future generations' resource consumption needs.

When considering the current Western world overindebtedness, social welfare prospects and climate change, we are already behind the schedule when it comes to fundamental foresighted preparedness. The following call for intergenerational leadership thus targets at contributing to eternal equity. Contemporary unprecedented intergenerational equity constraints, such as overindebtedness, pension reform of an aging Western world population as well as climate change demand for implementing intergenerational fairness. A human-imbued drive towards intergenerational conscientiousness comprising of social responsibility and future-orientation is argued as the basis of legal foundations, public policies and regulation that enables intergenerational justice over time. In addition, eternal equity can also echo in bottom-up participatory democracy and social representations of care between generations (Puaschunder, 2015d).

The following monograph, therefore, advocates for an interdisciplinary understanding of innovative applications of social economics for the alleviation of intergenerational imbalances. The book is targeted at distinctively advancing the readers' understanding of contemporary intergenerational equity infringements. For academia, the information conveyed may spearhead the idea of intergenerational equity as a natural behavioral law to provide a basis for future legal codifications. For practitioners, the recommendations may aid intergenerational fairness implementation strategies.

Overall, introducing intergenerational equity as a natural behavioral law advances the legal case for codifying intergenerational fairness on an international basis. Applying bounded ethicality onto financial and environmental considerations fortifies interdisciplinary behavioral law and economic models to aid on financial market predicaments, social welfare reform, and environmental threats. Exploring contemporary intergenerational constraints allows testing the generalizability and moderators of intergenerational conscientiousness experimentally. Investigating cognitive facets of intergenerational decision-making innovatively guides the financial, social responsibility, environmental protection education, and social welfare implementation. Enhancing financial, social conscientiousness, social welfare, and environmental protection through future-oriented and socially responsible public policies and economic market approaches is aimed at alleviating future predictable economic, social and environmental crises serving the greater goal to ensure a future sustainable humankind.

With the following monograph focusing on the present and near future regarding an unprecedented intergenerational equity kink starting from the turn of the 21st-century turn of the millennium, the book pursues the greater goal of freeing from short-termism shackles and grant wings of wisdom for our children, grandchildren, and great-grandchildren. Faith in future liberty grounded on noble munificence over time will acknowledge constancy of our children's freedom, economic prosperity and access to global common goods in a favorable environment. Socially responsible intelligentsia about the future of tomorrow's citizens of the world will pave the road to justice, foresighted vigilance seed the victory of eternal equity sparkled in our fin-de-millénaire.

2. 1. Overindebtedness

Economic and financial crises evolved as long as monetary systems exist. The current overindebtedness, however, is an unprecedented phenomenon resulting from conservative politics and the economic turmoil starting from 2007. In the last 30 years, libertarian trends have led to debt accumulation. Globalizing financial hubs dismantled taxation to attract capital from around the world.

Since the 1980's the finance world became detached from the real economy. Financial markets found value-at-risk and industrial values encroached financial matters. Money became a speculative good in free market economies. As bankers turned from service agents to risk hunters, risky banking overruled client services. Market actors were pushed to think short term and live on credit.

Undermined financial market fundamentals led to economic imbalances and collapsing financial institutions from 2007 on. In the aftermath of the 2008/09 World Financial Crisis, unfeasible lending business models heralded liquidity crunches. Surreal financial assets, speculations leaping over the market and irrational goals of a fast-paced financial community opened gaps between the economy and society. Financial market bailout at the real economy's expense incurred unprecedented governmental expenditures shrinking future economic prospects and social welfare opportunities.

While a neo-liberal finance elite gained value at risk at the expense of the general populace, also societal decision-making neglected future perspectives. People spent first then paid. Debt became dissociated from public shame. Borrowing overruled producing. In combination with tax income lows, nation states began to live beyond their means. National spending exhausted savings. Traditionally balanced budgets faded. While in the Western world public debts had already started piling up around the end of the millennium, the enormous bailouts of financial market exaltation in the aftermath of the 2008/09 World Financial Crisis left Western world governmental budgets constraint. Financial market downturn fueled a spiral of overindebtedness that will have to be paid back by decades of generations to come.

Future generations will sustainably be burdened due to our current short-term expenditures requiring debt repayments. Future prospects are hard to estimate as for being directly influenced by the overall growth rate. However, our current indebtedness is higher than the economic growth, and debt will transfer into the future – estimated 60% debt of GDP will be 90% of the GDP in ten years with long-term implications for the real economy and society. Some countries already face over 80% debts of the GDP to carry over to future generations prospected to be paid back by the next two generations. When debt rises faster than economic output, higher taxation lowers governmental freedom to provide social services heralding challenging governmental-citizen relations. On the international level, the public debt problem trades off from the international sovereignty of countries.

As a remedy in response to the crisis, since 2008 sweeping financial market regulation reforms were put in place in the Western world. The responses to the 2008/09 World Financial Crisis differ throughout the world – for instance, neo-liberal and post-Keynesian European economies invested in social welfare to avert the negative impacts of liquidity constraints on the populace, nurture equality and long-term financial values. American banks refraining from European transatlantic investments make the refinancing of commercial banks more expensive. In a self-fulfilling prophecy, this will shy liquidity. Combined with stricter policy programs in Europe and North America, impacted economic cycles reduce the likelihood of fast and easy budget supply, potentially leading to an additional rating downgrading, making refinancing more expensive and implying hard-to-controllable institutional hesitancy to cooperate. Further triple-A rating status will exacerbate austerity plans as for lowered governmental savings and heightened capital procurement costs. Speculations being financed at the risk of the real economy in bailouts brings along societal problems. Subsequent social welfare cuts steer civic upheaval as the occupy movement pointed out.

On the inner-European level, the Eurozone overindebtedness causes inevitable socio-political conflicts. The European political generation is pressured to implement a common bailout plan. European leaders, who had agreed upon the Euro as a common currency, now find themselves in a situation of asking who decides the fiscal policy in situations as with Greece and Brexit – and why was there no codification of default strategies and burden sharing clause in the inception of the Eurovision, which would be essential to lead the Eurozone bailout plans and retirement claims of Brexiters now?

Solutions on European soil are complex as European territories do not allow controlled inflation and in most parts still lack concerted, harmonized regulation. Banks are by now more likely to invest in international entities – foremost the European Central Bank – than inter-bank lending, especially after the 2012 EURIBOR/LIBOR scandal. The European monetary union stabilization pushes a regulatory Eurozone harmonization to ensure price and financial market stability. The Eurobonds solution as a major political leap forward of the European Union will have grand but mostly unforeseeable implications for the entire Eurozone that will leap over to other Western world market economies. An opening abyss of national monetary rescues and central banks dictating the Euro-bailout project currently couples political tension with nationalism and Eurozone fatigue.

The massive amount of expenses not only implies further economic turmoil and monetary instability but also trades off from social equity and fair resource distribution. Transferring debts into the future will lower future generations' access to education and social welfare. Debt burdens will fuel political frictions and psychological crises unprecedentedly pressure civilians. Current consumption rates in the aftermath of the financial crisis bailout burden sharing pile up debts to be dealt with in the future. Putting our current consumption paycheck in the child room causes liquidity problems for future generations with deep and lasting implications for personal investments and access to financial resources. Socio-economic problems arise within society foremost in the wake of governmental social welfare provision cuts. Older people who would have depended on bank insurance for income will have to rely on the governmental social welfare system. The young will experience equity downgrades in their investments – such as housing market drops – coupled with heightened unemployment risks. So, in the end, everyone on the age spectrum will be hit by the financial crisis as overindebtedness. Austerity plans touch all age groups. In-between age groups, the governmental overindebtedness will open vast generational gaps as in most industrialized countries financial debt carry-overs are imposed onto a ceasing body of children. Future shrinking wealth prospects are viciously coupled with a prospective lower body of productive workforce and taxpayers facing rising costs for a sophisticating health care and social welfare payments for a growing body of elder. Immigration could serve as a natural remedy to younger Western world populations (Puaschunder, 2016b).

2. 2. Demographic aging

Western world shrinking populations and diminishing economic power in the aftermath of the 2008/09 World Financial Crisis steer intergenerational pressures. Demographically declining populations lower the workforce to support a growing body of retired. While old and young have their expectations for a decent standard of living degraded in the aftermath of the 2008/09 World Financial Crisis, the economic situation leaves the young with having to afford their and the elderly's living. Life expectancy rising and stable pension ages coupled with ceasing populations will decline access to social welfare pensions and public health care.

Demographic changes open an intergenerational gap. Current major European, national pension systems appear unfeasible as the older are much better off. In some European countries, old fashioned taxation and pension plans have neither been reformed nor adjusted to aging populations for decades – for instance, while the Austrian living expectancy has risen over seven years since the 1950ies, the average pension age has decreased. Czech pensioners can receive 95-97% of their income after retirement while being allowed to work. Retired being able to double dip the market and governmental aid also enables to economically unfavorably bunker a workplace for the upcoming young.

As we tend to have promised too much regarding pensions for the future in the industrialized world, the young's ability and willingness to pay for the elder to maintain their lifestyles and standard of living is likely to vanish. Politicians currently face a massive redistribution conflict from the shrinking body of young and current budgetary liquidity constraints narrowing resources to pay for current needs. As Western world pensions have been promised to generously in the past, reforms need to pay attention to demographic changes through legislations and regulations that lift future generations' welfare expenditures burden. The current young will be the first generation that will experience drastic pension cuts and left not having as good pensions as expected. However, the pension system needs to be made feasible in a precautionary way so that social welfare and public wealth remains.

The current financial crisis and governmental overindebtedness add additional tension within the 2008/09 World Financial Crisis-shackled Eurozone. Subsequent credit rating downgrades put pressure on governmental social welfare provision flexibility. Structural problems from demographic shifts and non-adjusted pension systems lead to budget constraints. In Eurozone multilateral negotiations, national interest still prevails and frictions arise within the Euro compound. Civilians from one country with higher pension age should not be obliged to bail out a country with younger pensioner ages. It appears unfair if in one European country pensions get cut for 60-year olds in order to pay 50-year old pensioners.

If in Eurozone countries the European Union determines a responsibility to help – like Germany leading the bailout of Greece – the European circle must also put reasonable, transnational policies and a fiscal union in place. While young voters should try to change the societal wealth distribution, older – as the largest and most politically active voting group – are overrepresented to express democratic will. With more elder in the voting booth, who are on the receiving ends of pension benefits, the democratic outcomes tend towards their favor. The prevailing hegemony of the old not only features power and status being attributed to older people in parliamentary and policy circles but also the corporate and finance sectors being dominated by the elder. Most European populations have reached a tipping point with a ceasing chance of social welfare pension reforms. In the Western world, and especially in Europe, the chances are getting scarce or have even passed for democratic social welfare and pension system reforms. With the age pyramid already having tipped in most European countries, by now there is resistance to address pension reforms by politicians who struggle getting a political majority vote on pension readjustments. Taking given pension promises away from 'grayers' – the strongest political lobby – in a loss-avert world, by now equals political suicide. This occupation of the old is also problematic if the older generation blocks innovation and hinders the constructive progress of the young.

The European youth being confronted with a grim outlook and their political will not be enacted due to their shrinking populace leads to social unrest. Nationalism evolving within the Eurozone needs to be controlled and monitored with cautious attention. While history will not repeat itself, we must learn from the after-WI depression era, in which nationalist youth movements led to disastrous political regimes.

Individual pensions will require the citizen to pay for themselves, which will drive down solidarity in the social compound. Solidarity will also break apart when shrinking families lower the young generation's potential to take care of the old within the family compound. The generational pact must be maintained and the new generations' willing to contribute to a system that disproportionally pays for the old strengthened. The United Kingdom is the first EU country tackling the pension reform heralding difficult debates on burden sharing predicaments, which potentially played a role in the recent Brexit referendum decision. The intergenerational all-party parliamentary group must examine social contracts between age groups to curb infeasible social welfare transfers. In the meantime, environmental conditions are likely to change.

2. 3. Climate change

Resources like air, oceans, and water are prerequisites for life. Global common goods are globally linked and accessible for anyone – but owned by no one. No nation can claim common goods and declare sole access to common goods by itself. Distribution of global common goods has led to legal considerations ever since as fair access to global commons serves as the basis for peace and stability. But fair, equal and free access is getting harder in the age of globalization leveraging common goods problems into international dilemmas given unprecedented levels of interconnectedness and ecological pressures. Since the measurement of sustainability, energy consumption reached an all-time high in 2010 raising energy procurement costs and resource shortage. Since the recording of glaciers, arctic ice melting was highest during the last decade.

Rules of global access and use of global common goods are captured in international laws. Global common conscientiousness and solidary sharing of resource preservation are an ethical imperative of sustainable development. In the international compound, nation states have common but differentiated responsibilities in their differing contributions of global environmental acquisition. Common responsibilities comprise an equal share of environmental protection costs.

In the eye of current production levels leading to ecologic decline, all nations of the world will have to come together and form a global thinking on fair access to global common goods. Fair access to global common goods will alleviate global emergent risks as the core of international security politics and sustainable development. Common goods prevention and security of global resources will be the basis of societal advancement of a sustainable humankind.

While the ecological sensibility towards the environment has improved in the last 30 years and the Western world appears to have established a basic understanding of the scarcity of resources and the social responsibility to protect the earth; the threat of climate change implies novel and lasting environmental decline for humankind. By now, there is strong evidence of the anthropogenic contribution to climate change if men not even being the main offset trigger.

Today's climate impacts vary from country to country but impact on the entire planet. The Global Humanitarian Forum security report claimed already 300 million people being affected by climate change and the total economic expenditures of climate change having reached over 100 billion USD. The people suffering from climate change are expected to rise to 600,000 and the total annual economic costs will hit 300 billion USD within the next decade. In 20 years from now, the deaths caused by natural catastrophes arising with climate change could reach 500,000 civilians per year (Boscov-Ellen, 2015).

Climate change will determine the way people are living. Climates change precipitation patterns and access to water put agricultural and food preservation at stake. The melting of ice shells will unchangeably raise sea levels. Slugging and storm circuits will lead to natural disasters. The ecosystem and biodiversity are expected to diminish. Health risks, such as malnutrition, water problems, and diseases will spread. Climate refugees will be forced to leave behind their land, ancestry and cultural identity when about 200 million climate refugees will have to move in low-sea level lands prospected around the next decades (Puaschunder, 2017f). An estimate of 1,500 islanders will soon have to be evacuated from small islands in the South Pacific to larger islands and higher territories. The warming of ocean water will create hurricanes imposing danger on around 4 billion people in the United States alone. But also Inuit in the Arctic will have to move because of a massive ice melting.

Indigenous poor communities, who are already pushed to marginal levels of land, are going to be worst affected. African tribes will have to leave villages due to the impact of drought in central African regions, where seasons have been scarce for a decade. For instance, the Horn of Africa has just had the hottest years in succession ever reported. Severe droughts have also struck Kenya, Ethiopia, and Somalia, where attention is drawn to all time high food prices resulting in thousands of children starving. Climate justice will become an issue of concern when the major implications of a heating earth will be apparent and scarce resources vanishing potentially lead to violent frictions.

The populations most at risk, who live in the poorest regions of the world, are prone to be hit hardest by climate change, although they are neither emitters nor central to the political discussions or part of the solution (Puaschunder, 2017a). At the international level, common goods consumption and preservation breed inequality if the lifestyle of some is trading off from the environmental conditions of others. The Global West appears to cause an unfair impact on human-made climate change (Puaschunder, forthcoming b). The developed world is estimated to be responsible for 99% of carbon consumption, which raises strong global justice questions. Less than 1% of the greenhouse gas emissions that caused global warming is offset by 15 of the poorest nations – including the Middle East, Southeast Asia, Sub-Saharan Africa and small islands developing states (Puaschunder, 2017f). People in the poorer regions will go on the street and fight for their rights in the eye of missing future orientation or social equity regarding current ecologic problems.

At the same time, a positive relation between those countries that will economically benefit from a warming earth and Greenhouse Gas (GHG) emissions is found. Puaschunder (forthcoming b) investigated the relation between GDP growth prospects in light of climate change and percentage of GHG emissions reported by the Paris COP 21 Parties to the Convention.

Over a sample of 181 countries of the world, a highly significant correlation between economic winners of a warming earth and the self-reported percentage of GHG emissions for ratification was found. This result leads to the conclusion that those countries that emit more GHG are the ones with a positive economic prospect on the warming earth until 2100. The more time countries seem to have in a favorable climate for production, the more they are also likely to emit GHG and hence contribute to global warming. These results underline the need for attention to climate justice around the globe (Puaschunder, forthcoming a).

In the light of irreversible environmental decline, the time is ripe to reflect on intergenerational justice to avert an environmental decline in a cost-effective way (Puaschunder, 2017e). Our current consumption patterns should not transfer environmental debts to our ancestors or jeopardize the environmental conditions of our future children. The urgent need to address climate change is attributed in annual UN framework discussions leading to international agreements (e.g., the Montreal Protocol) and the inception of multi-lateral climate change aversion programs. The humanitarian dimension of climate change is central to the formal negotiations emphasizing mitigation and security. The international focus is placed on emerging economies – such as China and India – as the countries with the highest levels of CO_2 emission. Systems of monitoring, reporting, and verification of emissions are discussed to be installed to reduce emissions in non-binding agreements based on individual country pledges. While voluntary climate change aversion has been established during the last few years, it remains unclear how strong the commitment will be. The success of voluntary agreements depends on Western leadership and the consent of all countries around the world. Many of the more difficult issues were concerned in Durban in late December 2011 and the Rio+20 Conference. UN agencies, governments or developed and developing nations, corporations, foundations and constituency groups, who increasingly highlight the humane consequences of climate change, also organize debates.

Women take on a special role in averting climate change as female traits distinguish for traditional nurturing, environmental conscientiousness and emotionally laden family values. On women, who are also among the world's poorest given existing gender inequalities; climate change ultimately places a greater burden. Women – as primary food producers and water suppliers for their families – are affected by climate change because of the roles expected of them and the demands placed on them by their families and relatives. Not only are female prone to be dealing with the effects of climate change on the local ground but also is there a strong gender impact on climate change mitigation. International climate change awareness conferences have been led by female chairs (e.g., Cancun, Copenhagen, Denmark, Durban and South Africa) but also the Secretary-General of Climate Negotiations and the European Climate Change Commissioner are women. The Mary Robinson climate justice initiative promotes an alliance of women leaders on environmentalism and advocates for future meetings incepting a platform of female leadership on climate change aversion. The Rio+20 Conference featured a 'Women Creating a Sustainable Future' Board to pledge for intergenerational climate justice concerns. These female leaders have embraced a wider stakeholder group that climate change entails.

2. 4. On the social representations of intergenerational equity

Social Representations describe the genesis of collective ideas and allow predictions about future behavior of social masses during economic upheaval. Social representations shed light on the collective changes of people's mindset in times of crisis, during which people are more willing to talk and express their perceptions spontaneously. Based on associations at specific moments in history, social representations give access to lively reflections and collective moods arousing from current world events. Stemming from amalgamated individual perceptions of mutually shared and collectively discussed phenomena; social representations inform about public opinions and social norms. Social representations thereby allow delineating dynamic processes of socio-economic adaptation through capturing discourse and knowledge-exchange in the social compound (Kirchler, 2007).

Through the study of social representations, information about the diffusion of ideas and common societal knowledge on the prevailing Zeitgeist can be obtained (Durkheim, 1898; Moscovici, 1961). Social representations emphasize the shared social construction process when individuals try to make sense of external shocks and society collectively debriefs shared events. Social representations thus provide insights into the homogenous social perception of a shared environment. As for depicting societal reactions to economic influences over time, social representations grant orientation in times of change (Moscovici, 1984). As expressions of social perceptions of socio-economic transition, studying social representations allows to predict future behavior of social masses and forecast collective societal trends (deRosa, 1994; Moscovici, 1984; Nisbett & Ross, 1980).

In the past, the social representations were collected during the introduction of the European currency to measure the societal receptivity of a novel currency (el Sehity, Hoelzl & Kirchler, 2005). The social representations of experts on the global competency of the U.S. citizenry were retrieved by the U.S. Department of Education in early 2008 in order to respond to internationalization challenges in the era of globalization (de Sam, Dougan, Gordon, Puaschunder & St. Clair, 2008). Financial Social Responsibility social representations held by the finance community were obtained at the New York Financial District right before the outbreak of the 2008/09 World Financial Crisis (Puaschunder, 2010).

Next generations' debt, unfeasible social welfare and sustainability threats and intergenerational equity have to be addressed as an urgent topic of concern. Understanding intergenerational equity in the aftermath of the 2008/09 World Financial Crisis appears to open opportunities to implement financial, social responsibility, social pension reforms, and ecologic sustainability to respond to contemporary intergenerational equity demands.

While intergenerational equity concerns are as old as humankind – the 2008/09 World Financial Crisis, an aging Western world population, and climate change have put a new stance on the irreversible destruction of future prospects. Capturing the Zeitgeist on intergenerational conscientiousness in the aftermath of the 2008/09 World Financial Crisis contributes to our understanding of the societal process of sense-making when an unfamiliar external shock comes down on society.

During a European future conference in the late summer of 2011, opinions of international experts, leaders, practitioners, and students on 'Justice: Responsibility for the Future' were retrieved in order to delineate the contemporary social representations of intergenerational equity, the impact of the 2008/09 World Financial Crisis on intergenerational equity, environmental intergenerational equity concerns, and intergenerational equity implementation strategies.

By comprising a broad range of stakeholders and professions that hold differing notions on the topic of interest, who propose intervention strategies based on their own experience and professional backgrounds, social representations offered a broad societal spectrum to understanding economic phenomena's impact on social masses. The social representations collected thereby provide insights into the subsequent public choices and policy decision-making. The rationale behind using inductive reasoning and the free association method was to capture broad and diverse contents of multiple stakeholders.

The exploratory character of free associations was meant to most authentically snapshot a given point in time and hold the prevailing Zeitgeist on the topic of interests. The social representation interpretation then allows outlining stakeholder specific nuances of the topic of concern. The clear merits of the method and material are the authentic nature of the easily collected responses. The access to impressive elite insights and the reflexive nature of the debated associations provide first-hand, real-world insights on the topic of interest at the pulse of time.

The social representations of intergenerational equity were therefore retrieved from 110 speeches, interviews and conversations with leaders at a European future conference during the late summer of 2011 (Puaschunder, 2015d). A study of the social representations on intergenerational equity aimed at capturing leaders, experts, practitioners and students' concern about intergenerational balance, the impacts of the 2008/09 World Financial Crisis on intergenerational equity constraints, environmental, intergenerational equity concerns regarding climate stability as well as intergenerational equity implementation strategies. Free associations were collected at an international future conference in Europe during August 18 and September 3, 2011, by recorded speeches, panel discussions, and conversations made available by the conference administration. The conference setting was chosen as an information exchange portal that provides access to insider information in discussion forums on mind-framing, critical societal events. In the light of the aftermath of the 2008/09 World Financial Crisis, the three-week long gathering turned into hotspots for discussing regulation and innovative strategies to combat the crisis' negative impacts of socio-economic fallouts.

The future conference brought together the collective associations of leaders, experts, practitioners, and students, who reflected on the current state of the world and about changes in the domains of economics, entrepreneurship, finance, government, management, media, and politics. Experts from academia, business, economics, finance, international organizations, media, politics, public affairs, and religion were chosen as for their abstract reflexivity about current world events. Leaders, experts, practitioners, and students are also prone to hold theory-based problem-solving skills, foresight and future-oriented expertise, which grants their decisions societal impetus. As knowledgeable role models with the potential to grasp complex topics and filter manifold information in a multi-faceted way, the experts chosen are believed to be well versed in finding creative solutions and effective intergenerational equity implementation strategies in the intergenerational equity domain.

Overall, more than 4,000 international experts and leaders participated. In the Tyrolean mountain village, the three weeks' convention explored current societal concerns in interdisciplinary dialogues, speeches, and discussions. Leaders, experts, academics, practitioners, and students gathered for 16 one-week seminars in a variety of academic fields with a practice-oriented focus. The international, interdisciplinary conference offered participants the opportunity to discuss current world affairs with renowned world leaders from academia, business, economics, finance, international organizations, media, politics, public affairs and religion. The records were made available to the public by the conference administration. A qualitative analysis of the shared expert opinions and exchanged information but also the promoted crisis recovery strategies led to a contemporary snapshot of the social representations on intergenerational equity in the aftermath of the 2008/09 World Financial Crisis with special attention to environmental constraints and future-oriented problem-solving strategies.

The 48,460-word transcript of associations on the topic 'Justice: Responsibility for the Future' was categorized by the author to abstract the prevailing Zeitgeist of intergenerational equity during the late summer of 2011. From 110 expert opinions publicly expressed at the future forum, the social representations of intergenerational equity concerns in the late summer of 2011 were retrieved.

In addition, the 48,460-word transcript of all collected associations was screened for contents that would answer the question 'What is the impact of the 2008/09 World Financial Crisis on Intergenerational Equity?' In total 112 associations expressed in 5,632 words of 35 experts, practitioners, leaders or students provided differing information on the impact of the 2008/09 World Financial Crisis on intergenerational equity.

The 48,460 words transcript of all collected associations was also screened for contents on environmental sustainability and environmental, intergenerational equity constraints. In total 153 associations in 11,980 words of 64 experts, practitioners, leaders or students provided information on environmental, intergenerational equity constraints.

Finally, the 48,460 words transcript of all collected associations was screened for contents on intergenerational equity implementation recommendations and eternal equity strategies. In total 398 associations in 27,141 words of 89 experts, leaders, practitioners, and students provided collective insights on intergenerational equity implementation strategies.

The overall conference theme 'Justice: Responsibility for the Future' evoked associations about intergenerational equity. From all audio-recorded conference material expressed at a future conference in Austria during the late summer of 2011, intergenerational equity related contents were retrieved by the author. Drawing from a 48,460 words-pool of free associations on 'Intergenerational Equity,' all sayings were ordered into a category system that was developed inductively by the author based on the underlying content of the associations. The 48,460 words formed 66 differing content categories. The social representations of the intergenerational equity of international leaders, experts, practitioners, and students were investigated by calculating the frequency of associations per category. The associations were then analyzed using frequency tables to capture the core elements of the social representations. The categories and frequencies of the associations on intergenerational equity ordered by absolute frequency are displayed in Figure 2.

Figure 2: Categories of associations about intergenerational equity

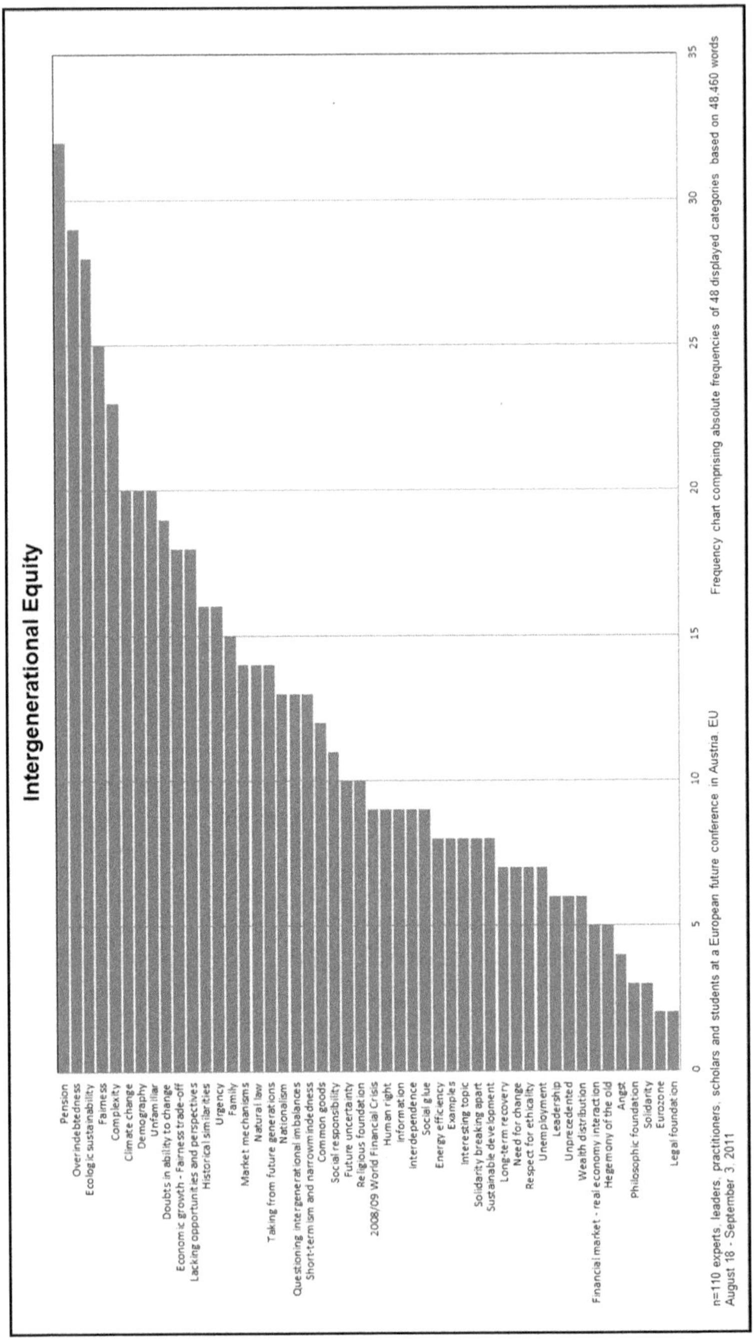

The most frequently mentioned associations on intergenerational equity form the categories 'Pension,' 'Overindebtedness,' 'Fairness' and 'Ecologic sustainability.' These associations on social welfare reform, overindebtedness, and ecologic sustainability are the core of the social representations on intergenerational equity during the late summer of 2011 captured at a European future conference. The semantic contents of the social representation on intergenerational equity during the later summer of 2011 revealed that international leaders are foremost concerned about intergenerational equity regarding unsustainable pension systems in the light of an aging and shrinking Western world population, overindebtedness in the wake of governmental deficit spending as well as ecologic decline stemming from climate change and unsustainable consumption patterns (see Figure 2). Overall, the social representations on intergenerational equity comprised of unsustainable pension systems in the light of aging, shrinking Western populations, overindebtedness in the wake of governmental deficit spending and ecologic decline related to climate change and unsustainable consumption. Stakeholder views of intergenerational equity included environmentalism on public officials' and international organizations' agendas. Politicians connected intergenerational justice to human rights.

The 2008/09 World Financial Crisis stressed focus on overindebtedness and uncertainty. Nationalism and protectionism were growing in the European finance and corporate worlds. Correspondence analyses outline the qualitative structures of the data. Mapping association categories along dimensions that describe the maximum of information based on frequency weighting represent the structure and relation between stakeholder groups and the retrieved categories (Greenacre, 2007). Figure 3 provides an outline of the nine subsamples Academia (n=32), Business (n=27), Economics (n=19), Finance (n=28), International Organizations (n=32), Media (n=32), Politics (n=44), Public Official (n=34) and Religion (n=28) in relation to the retrieved association content displayed in the 66 labeled association categories.

Figure 3 exhibits the two-dimensional solution in a correspondence chart mapping the nine expert groups in relation to the 66 categories derived from the mentioned contents on intergenerational equity. The correspondence chart in Figure 3 shows that environmental considerations are foremost on public officials and international organization representatives' agendas as they call for leadership on sustainable development. Politicians are starting to connect intergenerational justice to human rights. With the Eurozone reformation triggering Eurobond negotiations, national comparisons were on the minds of the finance and corporate worlds during the end of the 2011 summer. Media and academia representatives question intergenerational imbalances in the light of future uncertainty. There is a clear difference between financial economics groups and public officials' opinion on intergenerational equity. While the finance and economics elite reflected on topics around the Eurozone, overindebtedness and pension reform in the wake of demographic changes, public servants, and international organization executives are more concerned about sustainable development, energy efficiency and leadership on ecologic sustainability. The second dimension spans between business and academia as well as religion, which featured notions on religious and legal foundations, historical similarities but also ideas on solidarity and the social glue.

Figure 3: Correspondence chart of categorized free associations to intergenerational equity displayed by expert group (Source: Author)
Note: Sample size Academia (n=32), Business (n=27), Economics (n=19), Finance (n=28), International Organizations (n=32), Media (n=32), Politics (n=44), Public Officials (n=34), Religion (n=28)

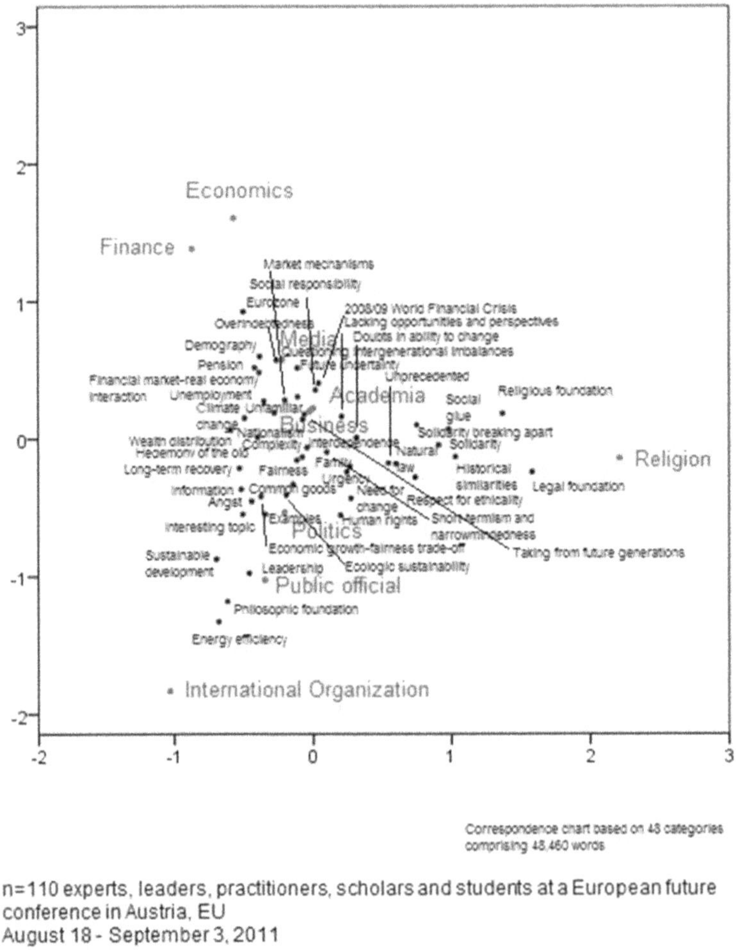

In total 112 associations comprising 5,632 words of 35 experts, practitioners, leaders or students provided differing information on the impact of the 2008/09 World Financial Crisis on intergenerational equity. The associations that would answer the question 'What is the impact of the 2008/09 World Financial Crisis on Intergenerational Equity?' were categorized based on their content in the same procedure as the social representations on intergenerational equity. The associations were categorized into a category system that was developed inductively by the author. The frequencies of associations per category were then calculated for every notion that held information on the impact of the 2008/09 World Financial Crisis on intergenerational equity.

The categories and frequencies of the associations of the experts, leaders, practitioners, and students are displayed in Figure 4 holding the frequencies of the association categories by experts, leaders and practitioners.

The most frequently mentioned associations addressed overindebtedness (f=15; 13.39%), uncertainty (f=9; 8.04%) and protectionism (f=9; 8.04%), which can be interpreted as the core of the social representations of changes in the perception of intergenerational equity in the aftermath of the 2008/09 World Financial Crisis of the respective stakeholders. Past short-termism has created urgent attention to long-term recovery through innovation and future investments. This hard and complex endeavor raises doubts about the ability to change. Solidarity, ethicality and social responsibility may help balance the economic growth versus fairness trade-off and nurture a more equitable and harmonious financial market-real economy interplay.

In total 153 associations comprising 11,980 words of 64 experts, leaders, practitioners, or students provided differing information on environmental, intergenerational equity constraints. The associations were assigned into a category system that was developed inductively by the author. The contents of the social representations of intergenerational equity environmental concerns were categorized and the frequency of the associations per category calculated for every association that would hold information on intergenerational equity environmental concerns. The categories and frequencies of associations on intergenerational equity constraints in the environmental domain are displayed in Figure 5.

On intergenerational environmentalism, experts, leaders, practitioners, scholars and students reflected ecological sustainability (f=20; 13.07%), climate change (f=17; 11.11%) and sustainable consumption (f=17; 11.11%). These most frequently mentioned associations are the core of the social representations of environmental, intergenerational equity notions of the respective stakeholders. Urgent environmental concerns require diversified energy efficiency. The prevailing categories also reveal that complex, interdependent common goods dilemmas demand global solutions.

International conferences, treaties, and vision councils legally back intergenerational justice, while family bonds aid real-world intergenerational conscientiousness.

Figure 4: Categorized free associations on the impact of the 2008/09 World Financial Crisis on intergenerational equity

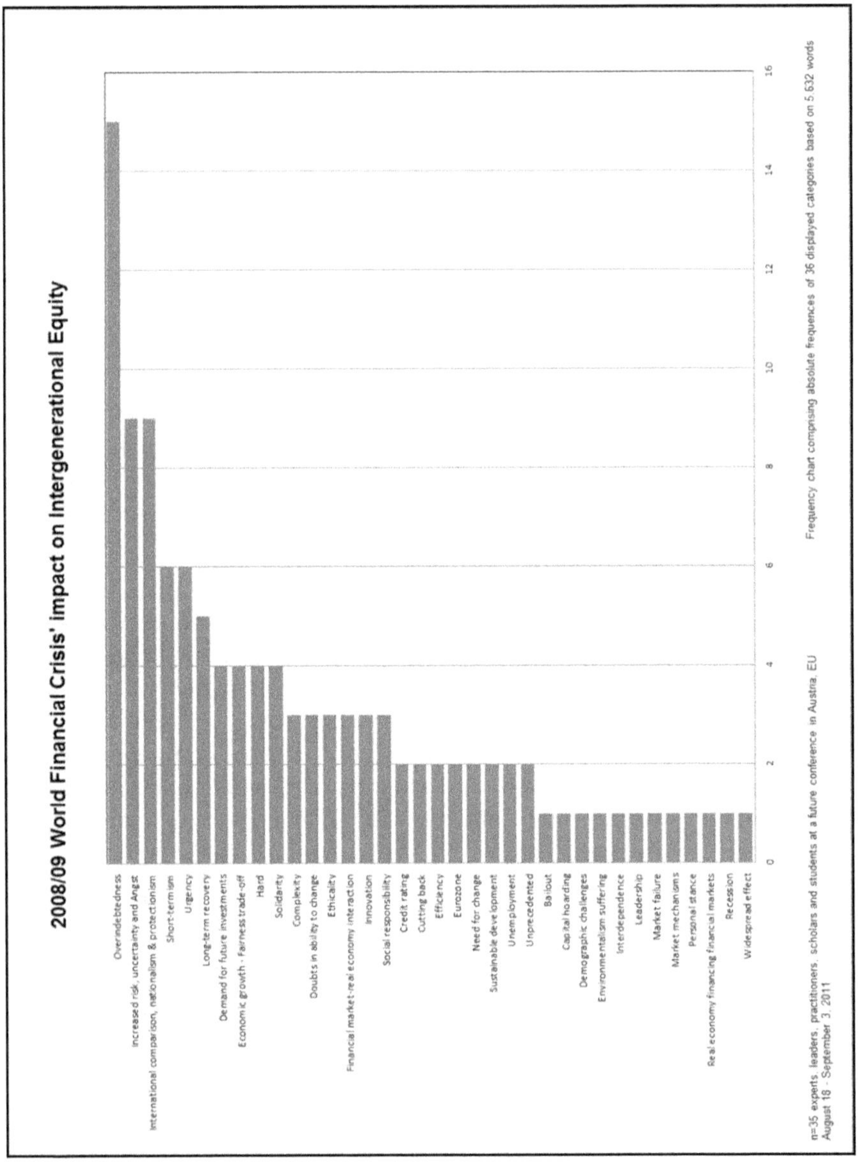

Figure 5: Frequencies of the associations per categories on intergenerational equity environmental concerns

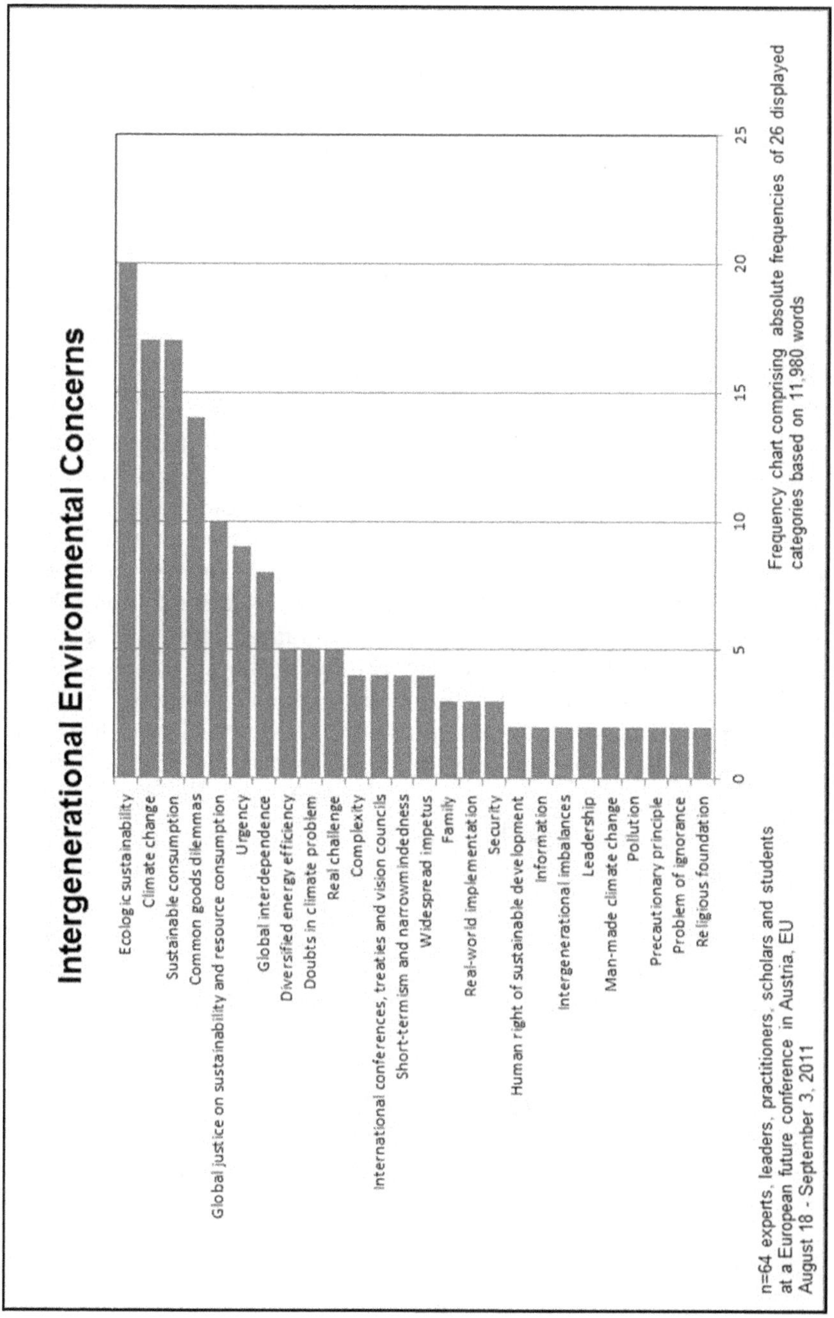

In total 398 associations comprising 27,141 words of 89 experts, leaders, practitioners, and students provided information on differing intergenerational equity implementation strategies. The contents of the social representations of the implementation of intergenerational equity were categorized. The associations were assigned into a category system that was developed inductively by the author. The frequency of associations in the association process was calculated for every notion that held information on intergenerational equity implementation suggestions. The categories and frequencies of the associations of the experts, leaders, practitioners, and students are displayed in Figure 6 holding the frequencies of the association categories.

For a successful implementation of intergenerational equity, experts, leaders, practitioners, and students suggested efficiency (f=20; 5.03%) and conscientious consumption (f=17; 4.27%). Long-term solutions (f=15; 3.77%) should comprise institutional regulation and foresighted taxation (f=15; 3.77%) balancing wealth, future investments in education and pension reforms.

Open debates will inform global leaders of complex intertemporal frictions and encourage them to find a global solution. International treaties and conventions will spearhead the codification of intergenerational justice as a human right. Innovation and economic growth through investments are market mechanisms to prevent future crises. Essential to eternal equity will be behavioral changes of citizens based – not only on ethicality and religious values – but also on the social glue featuring fairness from social responsibility and integrative solidarity. The codification of intergenerational equity must be pursued in international treaties and conventions. Leadership for institutional implementation but also social responsibility, religion, and ethicality play an important role in the expression of intergenerational fairness.

Promoting solidarity, ethicality and social responsibility but also innovations and future investment implement intergenerational equity. Long-term solutions may stem from institutional regulation and foresighted taxation but also open debates informing global leaders. A successful intergenerational equity implementation will feature efficiency, conscientious consumption and long-term solutions comprising institutional regulation and foresighted taxation but also future investments in education and pension reforms. Open debates will inform global leaders of complex intertemporal frictions and encourage them to find a global solution. International treaties and conventions will spearhead the codification of intergenerational justice as a human right. Innovation and economic growth through investments are market mechanisms preventing future crises. Essential to eternal equity will be behavioral changes of citizens based – not only on ethicality and religious values – but also grounded on the social glue establishing fairness from social responsibility and integrative solidarity.

Figure 6: Intergenerational equity implementation

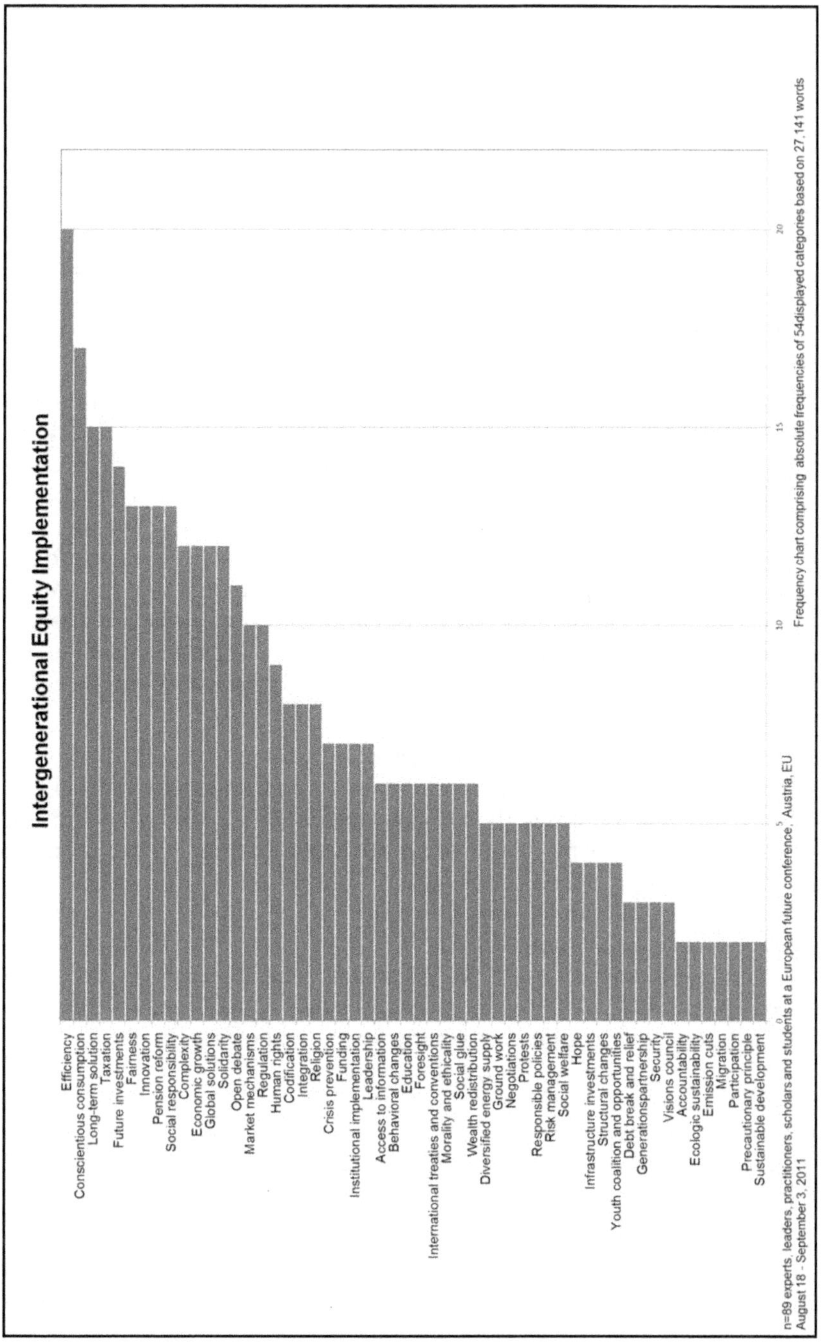

2. 5. Intergenerational equity as a natural behavioral law

The idea of intergenerational equity is as old as humankind. Conscientiousness for future generations is imbued in social customs and humane idealism. Intergenerational equity arises from the elderly wanting their offspring to prosper in at least as favorable conditions as experienced. Intergenerational equity is naturally felt, as parents do not want their child to grow up worse than they did themselves and thus improve the conditions for their offspring. This inner conscientiousness is related to morality that future children should find an at least as favorable standard of living as experienced. Whether it is the farmer or the forest caretaker, the small entrepreneur or the financial manager, we know we have to save for posterity and feel compassionate about future generations to come.

All major religions promote intergenerational equity values. The more religious people are, the more family members they have, and the stronger the ties between these family members, the more are they intergenerationally responsible. Religious roots describe the world being borrowed by current inhabitants, who must preserve the earth for future generations. Religious foundations advocate for the elder generation leaving the earth in an at least as good condition as found to their offspring. Judaism advises parents to plant trees for their children. The Old Testament's 4 Commandment advocates that children care for their parents. The Protestant church speaks about apocalyptic losses of living conditions. Islamic banking restricts speculative credit purchases in favor over real values. Indigenous principles outline one generation may not live at the expense of another.

The natural behavioral law of intergenerational equity was lived for centuries and transpired in the social compound as practiced in ancient, traditional customs. Already the oath of the ancient Athenian city postulates to 'transmit a city not only not less but better and more beautiful than it was transmitted' to ensure justice in-between generations. The Roman Law *prodigus*-clause excluded spendthrifts from economic interaction to save offspring from poverty and promote harmony between the young and old (Benke & Meissel, 2008). Intergenerational equity as a natural behavioral law is already described 700 BC by Hesiod in a son's concerns over inheritance. In the ancient Greek antique, Zeus symbolizes fatherly justice and eternal equity. In Cicero's 3rd book of 'De re publica,' justice is introduced as a natural law – a humane-imbued virtue that is fortified by the social compound and education. From the start of farming and property, inequity emerged, and throughout history, societies broke apart when they maintained on societal systems that were based on resource exploitation, leading to philosophers and writers advocate for equity over time.

Throughout history, intergenerational clashes fueled a revolt of the young versus the old. The post-World War I era featuring despair of the youth bred nationalism. European nationalist parties of the young had extremely negative consequences for the community – such as Adolf Hitler' s National Party rebelling against the 'Altpartei' or old party but also the roots of the communist opposition promoted themselves as a young force to build a pole against the old. The 1968 protests in Europe were an opposition against the old generation in the eye of ceasing economic stability given the oil and energy crises.

The inner hunch of intergenerational equality is grounded on a humane-imbued wish for fairness and an evolutionary offspring advantage if being brought up in socially-benevolent environments. Holding through time and place, natural laws of responsibility for the future are evolutionary-grown hunches stemming from compassion between overlapping generations. Evolutionary anthropologists trace first signs of social conscientiousness in between generations back to as soon as human would reach ages to experience 3-generation family members together. Since then elder, younger and youngest could directly transmit knowledge and crystallized wisdom from the old to the young. The rise in the stability of family ties and saliency of the eternal chain of life made generations feel for each other.

Intergenerational equity is a natural law in its roots and outcomes. Based on the evolutionary wish to improve the living conditions for descendants, intergenerational equity attributes the ethical obligation to provide an at least as favorable standard of living to future generations as enjoyed today. Intergenerational equity breeds an ethos of justice in-between current world inhabitants and future unborn averting imbalances between the young and elder. Natural laws determine decisions and drive actions in the social compound (Luf, 2011). As an implicit guide of day-to-day practiced common sense ethicality, natural laws are ethical anchors beyond regulatory frameworks and whimsical courtroom decisions (Mamor, 2010). In this feature, natural laws are a robust panacea to avert regulatory downfalls and oversight accountability challenges, as a human can orient their decisions during times of heightened uncertainty (Mayer, 2010).

Intergenerational conscientiousness as a natural care for offspring is transpired through social influences – for instance, externally nurtured by upbringing, education, role-model learning, and critical life events like parenthood but also external shocks coming down on society. Especially during times of crises, natural laws of fairness are in the focus of attention. External shocks and crises have always opened a window of opportunity to question the prevailing status quo, steering attention to human natural laws and ingraining social responsibility in society as external shocks bring people together to exchange information to control their world. Natural laws of inalienable rights have become prominent during revolutions and societal upheaval, in which inner moral compasses serve as a human imbued anchor of stability beyond legal frameworks and policy guidelines. For instance, in the aftermath of the 2008/09 financial meltdown, experts were quick to demand social responsibility in financial markets and less than 24 hours after the 2011 Japan nuclear disaster, newspapers addressed intergenerational conscientiousness.

Globalization, political changes, and societal trends have currently leveraged the societal demand for addressing intergenerational responsibility. Today we face unprecedented intergenerational challenges of an aging, over-indebted industrialized world reaching ecological limits regarding climate change, nuclear outbreaks, and biodiversity decline that put pressure on future generations (Barnosky, Matzke, Tomiya, Wogan, Swartz, Quental, Marshall, McGuire, Lindsey, Maguire, Mersey & Ferrer, 2011).[5] Today's most pressing intergenerational dilemmas of aging, indebtedness Western populations facing ecological challenges call for intergenerational equity. Intergenerational equity as a natural law remains hardly codified, as – apart from cyclical economic changes and historical wartime eras – living conditions have always overall been improving. While turning to natural laws to investigate intergenerational equity appears as the appropriate means to address these novel challenges; little is known about real-world intergenerational conscientiousness decision-making.

A preliminary literature review revealed a limited scientific investigation of intergenerational equity and a missing comprehensive framework of current intergenerational predicaments. Empirical intergenerational conscientiousness studies are rare. Classic economic models neglect intergenerational fairness as socio-psychological notions are hardly addressed in rational decision-making models. Understanding intergenerational conscientiousness, however, could help lowering tensions arising between the old and young in the eye of future prosperity threats. New economic thinking may integrate behavioral aspects and innovatively leverage our idea of intergenerational equity as a natural behavioral law in order to implement eternal equity and ensure harmony over time.

---

[5] http://wwf.panda.org/about_our_earth/all_publications/lpr_2016/

Chapter 3

Intergenerational Balance

3. 1. Intergenerational mobility

In overlapping generations' models, representative agents live a finite time overlapping with another agent's lifespan. Individual's lifetime utility is a function of consumption in all periods (Allais, 1947). Individuals live for two periods as young (period 1) and old (period 2). In every period, there are old and young living together, and there is constant population growth (Samuelson, 1958). Individuals receive an endowment of goods at birth that endures for one period, whereas money endures for multiple periods (Diamond, 1965). The endowment of goods throughout lifetime depends on the endowment of labor creating real income while people are young and the natural endowment of inheritance based on ancestor's wealth and transfers. The model allows for oversavings of the old generation, and the young generation can accept money from the previous old in exchange for consumption with the prospect of using that money to purchase consumption when they are the old generation. For intergenerational improvement of opportunities over time, concurrently living generations have to engage in social interaction.

Social environment and human capital formation are necessary yet overlooked factors determining intergenerational advancement (Borjas, 1995). Social environments lead to the agglomeration of opportunities through social interaction but also create poverty trap holes that individuals cannot leave (Durlauf, 2001; Goldberger, 1989). Intergenerational stickiness was found in housing zones determining education, marital fulfillness, and wages over time (Chetty, Hendren & Katz, 2015; Osborne, 2002). The environment during childhood appears as a key determinant of an individual's long-term prospects of societal status (Bouchard & McGue, 1981; Chetty et al., 2015). The driver to break intergenerational persistence through intergenerational mobility lies in intertemporal merit-based advancement opportunities.

Thomas Piketty's (2014) Capital in the 21st Century is about societal inequality. The trend of the rise of the super-rich that can be traced back to power, resources, taxes, financial markets and the social dynamics of the top 1% raises questions regarding social mobility (Volscho & Kelly, 2012). Meritocratic intergenerational mobility is at the core of equitable societies (Arrow, Bowles & Durlauf, 1999).

Inequality persists in immobile societies as indicated by the r=.56 88, p<.05 correlation between inequality and intergenerational wage persistence (OECD, 2010). Intergenerational mobility is a feature of equal societies across countries.[1] Inequality diminishes when people improve their societal placement from one generation to the next (Cooper, Durlauf & Johnson, 1994). Intergenerational equity grants equity of chances – not outcomes, which should be merit based – over time for this generation and the following (Loehlin & Nichols, 1976). If individuals cannot advance based on their education, work, and natural skills, then their social status is determined by their parents' and ancestors wealth, income and networks (Becker, 1988; Bowles, Gintis & Osborne, 2008; Menchik, 1979). Individual ability and ambition appear as fairer determinants of one's place in the social order and, from an economic perspective, merit-based allocations appear more productive over time as for being based on long-term intelligence and values, such as the need for achievement (Arrow et al., 1999; Becker & Tomes, 1986).

Yet, inequality persists in immobile societies (Erikson & Goldthorpe, 1992). An OECD (2010) Economic Policy Reform Report outlines a r=.5688, p<.05 correlation between inequality and intergenerational wage persistence, measured by the gap between the estimated wage of an individual whose father had achieved tertiary education and the wage of an individual whose father had below upper secondary education (Solon, 1992, 1999; Taubman, 1976).

Across countries, intergenerational mobility is a feature of equal societies.[2] Meritocracy and access to education are prerequisites for intergenerational mobility. Gary Becker and Richard Posner (2012)[3] therefore recommend that governments provide first-class education and social services to gifted, yet underprivileged children.[4] Social welfare spending helps reduce education gaps for students from disadvantaged backgrounds by up to 42.9 percentage points (Ashenfelter & Krueger, 1994; OECD, 2010).

However, OECD economists find government-funded higher education and merit-based scholarships do not entirely reduce unfair favoritism of privilege (OECD, 2010). Instead, intergenerational immobility persists. Parental

---

[1] http://www.conferenceboard.ca/hcp/details/society/intergenerational-income-mobility.aspx

[2] http://www.conferenceboard.ca/hcp/details/society/intergenerational-income-mobility.aspx

[3] http://www.becker-posner-blog.com/2012/06/capitalismposner.html

[4] http://www.becker-posner-blog.com/2012/12/meritocracy-social-mobility-intergenerational-mobilityposner.html

backgrounds influence student achievement in secondary education by up to 63 gradient points in the PISA Score.[5] Children of uneducated parents are three times less likely to start tertiary education, facing an overall intergenerational persistence of 66.7 percentage points. Surprisingly, intergenerational immobility remains around 20-30 percentage points, even in countries with anonymous student bodies. Children from parents with academic backgrounds also benefit from a wage premium of up to 20%, compared to those growing up in non-academic households (Atkinson, Maynard & Trinder, 1983; Corak & Heisz, 1999). The link between individual and parental earnings ranges from 15 to 50% intergenerational earnings elasticity across OECD countries (Charles & Hurst, 2002; Mazumder, 2008). Harvard Professor Robert Putnam (2015) therefore argues that people might not overcome their parent's social economic status because societal class creates and molds one's expectations for success and ability (Mulligan, 1997). Living in a society with little merit-based opportunity reinforces low expectations for escape. Education may not make sense if there is no hope for merit-based mobility (Osborne, 2002). Intergenerational advancement may thus only prosper in the wake of meritocracy, an overlooked prerequisite of societal equality.

While economists can improve access to economic market opportunities,[6] institutional policy makers can minimize discrimination, and global governance entities instigate intergenerational transfers, social scientists should focus on how to build societal trust in merit-based intergenerational mobility (Brasington, Kato & Semmler, 2010; Ghilarducci, 2005; Puaschunder, 2015b, e). Meritocracy as the psychological backbone of a fair society; together with hopeful trust in intertemporal improvement, are key drivers of economic productivity, opening an innovative path to a long-term equitable society.

Building on Thomas Piketty's (2014) *Capital in the 21st Century* that revolutionized economic thoughts on inequality, also the connection of inequality and equality representing agents within one societal system may alleviate the downsides of inequality. Started by the 2008/09 World Financial Crisis and cumulated in the subsequent Occupy movement, attention to rising inequality regarding economic wage, opportunity and wealth led to advocacy for a

---

[5] The Programme for International Student Assessment (PISA) is a worldwide study by the Organisation for Economic Co-operation and Development (OECD) in member and non-member nations of 15-year-old school pupils' scholastic performance on mathematics, science, and reading.

[6] http://www.nytimes.com/2015/05/05/upshot/why-the-new-research-on-mobility-matters-an-economists-view.html?abt=0002&abg=0

more equal society. Innovatively, a mixture of equality and inequality within a societal network is proposed. A complementary connection of equality and inequality could allow transfer of implicit wealth distributed merit-based. By the example of Ivy League educational institutions, but also elaborating on the social environment and interaction networks, a novel economic wealth transfer model could alleviate the societal problems associated with inequality (Puaschunder, 2015b, 2016c, 2017c). Within an economic system, dyads of *unequal* crystallized value based on heritage (e.g., royal families, legacy admits) and merit-based *equality* represented by offspring from families with underprivileged backgrounds, whose outperforming ambition, fluid intelligence, and drive may lead to fruitful social interactions and beneficial wealth transfers, may create beneficial economic outcomes. On the societal level, transformation networks of favorable environments may serve as social mobility hubs if entered merit-based by underprivileged families. Although inequality could be curbed through merit-based distributed value transfer opportunities, a blatant research gap on information about the direct and indirect transactions and interactions between equality and inequality representing agents within societal networks exists. Future research on the fruitful connection between inequality and equality represented in one societal setting should give hope in Piketty's outlook of rising inequality (Puaschunder, 2016c).

3. 2. The age of austerity

In response to the 2008/09 economic downturn, nations experiment with austerity, which restricts public spending but also lowers investments and thus may bleed into economic stagnation and prosperity decline. Overall, austerity as a cure is supposed to be worse than the disease as austerity economics may plunge countries into worsening unemployment, record poverty rates and growing civil unrest (Aja, Bustillo, Darity & Hamilton, 2013; Semmler, 2013). Curbing essential government spending on education, social welfare, public safety, retirement, health, and infrastructure slows economic activities and hinders recovery. The negative effects of austerity cuts are severe with estimated costs for the US between 1.25 and 1.75% of GDP in 2013 (International Monetary Fund, 2013). Austerity cuts in the Eurozone have led to reductions in overall output in excess of the total level of spending cuts. Austerity economics are making inequality worse due to austerity-driven cuts essential to public service (Aja et al., 2013; Howell, 2013; Pollin, 2013). Not only downplaying the importance of government spending neglects its multiplier effect on economic growth; but also will austerity induce recession like effects on economic growth (Marglin & Spiegler, 2013; Proaño, 2013) and destabilize nation states (Lawson-Remer, 2013).

In Europe, austerity measured bred inequality resulting in welfare losses and extreme decreases in workers' wages. In Greece, real wages fell by more than 30% since 2009, inflicting damages on social cohesion, living standards and the EU social model (Semmler, 2013). During this period of increasing financial stress and budget consolidation policy, the EU monetary union using the same currency led to weaker countries being unable to devalue their own currency, which might have stimulated their economies by increasing exports and debt repayment burden easing (Semmler, 2013).

Nations having no national central bank that can control the monetary policies of sovereign nations or a sufficient deposit insurance that might calm people who fear a banking collapse, led to countries' downward pressure on wages. Unprecedented credit expansion and active monetary policy resulted in fixed-rate full allotment of liquidity of banks on demand on its leveraged investment positions.

Longer-term refinancing operations were targeted at reducing uncertainty and encouraging banks to provide credit to the economy (Semmler, 2013). Regime-dependent negative austerity multipliers resulted in different value at different stages of the business cycle at different levels of financial stress and external indebtedness of the country. In Greece, high levels of austerity triggered a strong contractionary multiplier (Semmler, 2013). The strong downward effect caused high unemployment, more financial stress in the financial sector with increased credit and bond spreads, banking risks and falling internal and external demand (Semmler, 2013). For instance, Greek public consumption fell by 9.1%, which caused investment to fall by 20.7%, imports by 3.4%, private consumption by 7.1% and the aggregate demand by 7.1%. An austerity-driven reduction in spending had a stronger negative effect on output and employment when there was severe financial stress, which in turn reduced consumption and investment, feeding a downward spiral (Semmler, 2013).

Debt stabilization depends on complex regimes and the economic environment as described by financial stress, the vulnerability of the banking system, monetary policy and the state of internal and external demand, exchange rates and other factors. The level of aggregate expenditures and taxes are relevant as well as the composition of spending and taxes – if government money spending is in health, education, infrastructure and wages and salaries in the public sector, then the multiplier will trigger positive long run effects (Semmler, Greiner, Diallo, Rajaram & Rezai, 2011; Stein, 2011).

Hastily enacted EU austerity programs will have uncontrolled distributional effects and endanger the future of the EU welfare state (Boyer, 2012). In particular, social spending on the elderly hurts young people if retirement and elderly health care spending take funding away from investments supporting education and youth development (Ghilarducci, 2013). Support from spending on the elderly and the young are thereby seen as complements. Policies should thus focus on economic opportunity and foster a strong middle class to stabilize democracy (Lawson-Remer, 2013). Potential policy options include increasing tax revenues for social and infrastructure spending – e.g., through taxing top-income earners (Piketty, Saez & Stantcheva, 2011) – in contrast to spending cuts and debt budget plans in line with the Bowles-Simpson proposals (Washington Post, 2013). Austerity driven by controversial economic theory and politics can thus result in inadequate socio-economic downfalls yet without austerity there is the constant fear of bankruptcy. As a result, there is a deep division among economists on austerity linked to fundamental differences in morality over the ultimate purpose of economic and social policy rather than technical debates on methodology (Milberg, 2013). While the intellectual argument for austerity appears to be week, political forces behind austerity are strong (McGahey, 2013).

Austerity may deepen societal inequality and heighten the tensions and contradictions inherent in capitalist economies. We therefore need to explore a range of policy approaches that can reduce the level of risk for borrowers and lenders through governmental loan guarantee programs and raise the costs for banks to continue holding cash hoard (Dymski, 2013). The post-2008/09 World Financial Crisis liquidity trap – featuring zero-interest rate policies – is made worse if there is a fiscal austerity agenda instead of focusing on federal stimulus (Pollin, 2013). As an alternative, President Obama sought to stimulate the economy when he took office during the Great Recession but also targeted long-term debt reduction by creating the National Commission on Fiscal Responsibility and Reform in terms of the Bowles-Simpson Commission (McGahey, 2013). However, also the effects of stimulus are still highly debated. The neoclassical idea is that government expenditure crowds out private investment, so it will not be stimulatory in the long run. The Keynes-Kalecki-post-Keynesian position states that stimulus is fine up to full employment levels are achieved, when inflation may set in. In order for stimulus to have a lasting positive impact on output, employment and real wages, as well as the productivity of labor, must be raised so as to keep unit labor costs down.

Austerity measures should be revised for becoming more class targeted. A class focus could address austerity for the richer segments of society, in order to leverage a greater amount of funding while not harming high-risk communities at the lower income and wealth bounds of society. The implementation of such a class-sensitive austerity plan could be enacted through progressive taxation and focus on higher taxation for the wealthier societal segments. Such a strategy would curb the harmful societal implications of austerity and avoid long-term socio-economic downfalls.

3. 3. Climate stability bonds

Climate change accounts for one of the most pressing problems in the age of globalization as for exacerbating more risks than ever before in terms of water crises, food shortages, constrained economic growth, weaker social cohesion and increased security risks (Centeno & Tham, 2012; World Economic Forum Report, 2015). The implementation of climate stability is therefore the most challenging contemporary global governance predicament that seems to pit today's generation against future world inhabitants in a trade-off of economic growth versus sustainability. Current climate stability policies (e.g., cap & trade, carbon tax, green energy) outline that the burden of climate change aversion – including the cost of mitigation and adaptation – is unevenly distributed by falling mostly on the current generation. The excess burden for current generation has also been implicit in the work of the typical Integrated Assessment Model, IAM, (Nordhaus, 2008), the contemporary threshold as well as other mitigation and adaptation models, e.g., the social cost of carbon. Innovative intertemporal fiscal policy approaches (e.g., of Jeffrey Sachs, 2014) guide the development of a basic framework to study how an efficient and fair allocation of efforts towards mitigation and adaptation can be achieved.

In standard neoclassical economic models, climate change abatement is perceived as trading off from economic growth as for cost-cutting behavior. While classic economics portrayed balancing the interests of different generations as ethical problem of competitive markets requiring governance for intergenerational transfers and some economists even opposed discounting of future utilities (Allais, 1947; Harrod, 1948; Ramsey, 1928); climate change has leveraged intergenerational equity as contemporary challenge of modern democracy and temporal justice an ethical obligation for posterity.

In general, resources are balanced across generations by social discounting to weight the well-being of future generations relative to those alive today. Regarding climate justice, current generations are called upon to make sacrifices today for future generations by mobilizing low-carbon energy to cut carbon emissions to avert global warming (Sachs, 2014). Climate change mitigation at the expense of lowered economic growth seems to pit the current generation against future ones. Costly climate change abatement prospects are thus hindering currently necessary action on climate change given a shrinking time window prior to reaching tipping points that make global warming irreversible (Oppenheimer, O'Neill, Webster & Agrawal, 2011).

As a novel alternative to ensure climate justice, Sachs (2014) proposes to fund today's climate mitigation through intertemporal fiscal policies enabled by climate bonds financed through taxation faced by future generations. Climate stability bonds are introduced as a means of intergenerational climate change burden sharing strategy to elicit future-oriented climate stability for posterity. The current generation mitigates climate change and provides infrastructure against climate risk financed through climate bonds to be paid by future generations. Since for future generations the currently created externalities from economic activities – the effects of CO_2 emissions – are removed, this entails that the current generations remain financially as well off as without mitigation while improving the environmental well-being of future generations. As Sachs (2014) shows, this intergenerational tax-and-transfer policy turns climate change mitigation and adaptation policy into a Pareto improving strategy. Sachs' (2014) intergenerational burden sharing idea presents a 3-model climate change burden sharing through fiscal policy (with bond issuing) and reflects the implementation regarding contemporary finance and growth models with respect for maximizing the utility of the model. The current generation thereby mitigates climate change financed through bonds to remain financially as well off as without mitigation while improving the environmental well-being of future generations.

Jeffrey Sachs (2014) novel angle towards climate justice elicits future-oriented loss aversion, which leads to a fairer solution across generations. Shifting the costs of climate abatement to the recipients of the benefits of climate stability appears as a novel, feasible and easily implementable solution to nudge many overlapping generations towards future-oriented loss aversion in the sustainability domain. This powerful strategy instigates immediate climate change mitigation in an overall Pareto improving crisis management for all generations. While intergenerational burden sharing on climate change is a novel economically superior strategy and real-world relevant emergent risk prevention means (Centeno et al. 2013); we currently lack information on the impact of climate mitigation through debt on economic growth and the model's sustainability over time. Testing for the feasibility and sustainability will provide real world relevant means how to implement climate stability on a long-term scale. Studying the types of bonds issuing that would achieve such goals will help to explore the more complicated bond issuing practices involved. In this context, it should also be investigated if the climate change debt-adjusted growth model stays within the bounds of a sustainable fiscal policy.

This elementary but very innovative model by Sachs (2014) can be integrated into contemporary growth and economic climate models. Yet, unknown remains how climate bonds can actually be phased into climate policies to obtain socially optimal solutions. To solve, calibrate and test such a new model of climate change policies and to show that such a debt augmented growth model stays within the bounds of a sustainable fiscal policy, new methods like nonlinear model predictive control (NMPC), which solves complex dynamic systems with different nonlinearities for finite decision horizons, should be employed. Future research should also analyze micro- and macroeconomic insights on the well-balanced harmonization of climate change mitigation and adaptation in order to provide public policy recommendations.

Overall climate stability bonds offer to lead a well-balanced climate mitigation and adaptation public policy mix guided by macroeconomic analysis results. Shifting the costs of climate abatement to the recipients of the benefits of climate stability appears as a novel, feasible and easily implementable solution to nudge overlapping generations towards future-oriented loss aversion. Adding onto the contemporary idea and practice of climate bonds alongside providing incentives to channel funds into climate stability is recommended. Research in this area will also retrieve information on the harmonious interplay of climate change mitigation and adaptation in the public policy domain for ensuring a sustainable humankind.

Chapter 4

Intergenerational Equity Implementation

The implementation of intergenerational equity ensures that future generations enjoy at least the same choices if not better opportunities as prevailing today. Global challenges like demographic aging, climate change and sustainable development that cannot be solved on the national level demand for international leadership facilitating and structuring public engagement on common concerns. In top-down approaches, global consortia concertedly solve internationally interconnected common goods problems and work towards a common vision of global justice throughout the world. Sustainability councils – such as the UN 'Ombudsman for Future Generations' address intergenerational considerations and define intergenerationally-equitable goals based on normative ethics and procedural justice. Transnational democracy coordinates and sets solidarity standards of common goods preservation based on notions of fairness on equal opportunities and merit-based allocation of resources.

Legal writings inspire vision councils' understanding of intergenerational equity as a human right to development. Connecting intergenerational equity to human rights of life, liberty, and freedom, grants sustainability for future generations and equal access to common goods for humankind over time. At the Rio Conference in 1992 – the first global conference on sustainability providing the Rio Agenda 21 – first inferences were drawn between sustainability and human rights in the realization that responsibility for the future is a prerequisite of well-being for humankind. The following year in Vienna, human rights were referred to environmental sustainability. At the 10th anniversary of the 1992 Rio conference on sustainable development in Johannesburg, there was a clear coming together of sustainability and human rights.

The legal enforcement of intergenerational fairness is limited as future unborn are not able to sue their grandfathers for debts, request pension reserves today and avert environmental lock-ins. Top-down approaches may not give voice to future needs since constitutional experts not even agree on the rights of embryos, unborn are not present in courtrooms and lobbies do not advocate for future concerns. Legal frameworks and structural reforms must be accompanied by behavioral changes – such as education to efficiently use scarce resources, invest for the future and be conscientious of energy consumption – in order to overcome current intergenerational constraints. Societal frameworks featuring responsibility as respect for future generations and decisions at an early stage will lead to new forms of institutional governance determining the living conditions of following generations.

The intergenerational equity implementation requires a multi-stakeholder approach in which public and private sector forces increase productivity concertedly through technological advantages and social innovations. Equality of merit-based access to opportunity accelerates economic growth attuned to sustainability goals and social integration. Intergenerational justice on the operative level features foresight and socially responsible policies. Age-diversified juries, well-tempered investigation panels and Generationspartnerships foster information exchange between young and old. Through voting, the young partake in societal decision-making. Youth coalitions advocate for long-term decision-making in parliamentary circles – such as in the case of the German debt brake constitutionalized in 2011. In a participatory democracy, in which decisions are made publicly and discussed openly with people having a say in their solution, citizens decide more conscientiously of their children's need. The political communication on intergenerational equity implementation strategies may focus on easy understandable, personal examples that help to bring the present into the future and think in terms of own children and imagining the sustainability of their welfare. Such as it will be your children, who will not get a house because you used to earn more, cannot afford that extra education, will face higher levels of taxation and a longer working lives ahead while suffering from climate change. So, in the end, your children are not going to enjoy the same future as you had. Accompanied by peaceful democracy-in-action protests, this will lead people to think and give beyond their personal lives.

Bottom-up discussion platforms ingrain intergenerational perspectives in current decision-making. Generations coming together will allow discussing problems in the social compound. Open debates about commonly shared values and goals will clarify what public debt, pension welfare and environmental responsibility mean for future generations and leverage intergenerational equity into a uniting, politically driven issue. General discussions nurture consensus on societal problems of all age groups. Combining the old and young's perspectives in dialogues between generations helps paying attention to future generations' needs and balances between the young, who strive for novel change and the old, who pass on their wisdom of experience. New media technologies help bridging the young and old by granting access to information on the needs of all age groups. The current interconnectedness of the world thereby becomes a tool to embrace older people and include them in society so that they are more willing to save for their children, invest in the youth and pass on wealth rather than spending it on their current consumption. A harmonious representation of diversified viewpoints is gained in a dialogue between generations that integrates young and olds' viewpoints and represents all societal groups. Beyond legal and regulatory boundaries, partnerships between young and old encourage a culture of voluntary intergenerational fairness. Transfers of wisdom from the old to the young raises solidarity in the social compound and grants stability for the community whilst fostering positive social development and societal welfare.

Intergenerational equity as natural behavioral laws serves as an ethical anchor to steer behavior towards future-orientation and societal responsibility. Beyond legal contracts, family bonds and responsible education form prosocial, intergenerationally conscientious norms as a basis for a favorable societal climate. Education will lead people to feel obliged to invest in the upcoming young and see future allocations as societal progress. While the young should be brought up with intergenerational values, the elder should be taught to understand the needs of the young. Benefitting from the crystallized intelligence of the old, the young must drive technological and social innovations to change societal patterns. Change laboratories should focus on how to embrace moral codes of wealth distribution between generations. The family compounds should support the upcoming generations – for example with credits for long-term investments like housing and education in times when it has become more difficult to borrow from the banks as first-time buyers, and education has gotten more expensive.

Regarding overindebtedness, the public good of a stabilized economy depends on merit-based, fair asset allocation and risk management. Macroeconomic policy frameworks reduce risks in the interplay of financial markets and the real economy. Regulation must alleviate boom and bust related market downfalls and work towards a fair resource (re)distribution in accordance with societal values. After a pendulum swing from liberal to state interventionism backwards to neo-liberal ideas, well-tempered policy balance may feature anti-cyclical politics of credits, controlled inflation, debt brakes and debt cancellation. Creating economically favorable locations that attract international capital and sustainable projects that fortify potential vitalize the economy. Capital institutions focus on core activities away from value-at-risk seeking will establish lasting and sustainable relations with customers.

Social welfare provision constraints related to demographic changes can be solved by market productivity growth, wealth redistribution, pension reform and adjusted pension expectations. An efficiency increase of pension schemes targets at raising tax revenues, cutting social benefits and distributing pensions merit-based while paying attention to social welfare provision for those who cannot compete in economic markets due to natural disadvantages, e.g., handicaps. Inheritance tax redistributes wealth from the old to the young on the individual level, yet problematic appears that inheritance tax breeds inequality and has been ceased in most EU countries. People should be incentivized to belong to a certain tax group and remunerated according to their work productivity for society. Pay-as-you-go pension insurance could be considered as a market approach to solving social welfare problems of an aging population. Direct governmental transfers to underprivileged and tax breaks grant access to health and education. Structural reforms may ensure that the young have an at least as favorable standard as the old today by raising the pension age in accord with life expectancy. Increased pension ages, however, crowd out opportunities for the young to enter the workforce. Requiring pensioners by law not to work opens the market but puts productivity pressure on the young and strips crystallized expertise off the labor force. Pensioners should thus be encouraged to use their potential for the society of the labor market. Based on their expertise and former affiliations, healthy civilians may contribute to labor charity – similar to Norwegian welfare models or Kibbutz systems – to aid the sustainability of the pension scheme alongside providing engagement opportunities for the elder. Solidarity supporting pensioners based on social responsibility is a strong social welfare safety net. Aging populations-related social welfare crunches can also be curbed by migration overcoming reproduction gaps. Immigration, however, requires integration, education, and policies harmonization expenditures – especially throughout territories with differing languages and cultures like Europe. Migration should be pegged to the merit-based performance of immigrants.

Ecologically we must not live at the expense of future generations regarding natural resource consumption and climate change. As the market by itself is not long-term future-oriented or socially conscious, ecologic problems demand a political frame to implement foresight and governmental will to find a well-balanced resource distribution over time. Climate conscientiousness will require a modern, multi-cultural, multi-factual and urgent response to enact climate stabilization in the future. International consensus must ensure that large, emerging economies such as China and India inept systems of monitoring, reporting, and verification of emission reduction. Legislation backing intergenerational equity will leverage climate justice as a human right in order to alleviate global emergent risks of resource scarcity. Legal frameworks like international contracts define generational justice. Injustices and inequalities created by present world inhabitants must be treated as human rights abuses and addressed by international institutions – like The United National Environmental Program. International cooperation and regional collaborations on the preservation of global common goods comprise a coordinated action to ensure fair usage of global common goods in accordance with international laws as a prerequisite of security and basis for the socio-economic development of sustainable humankind. Contracts with precautionary principle attribute common but differentiated responsibilities to enable sustainable development and common goods preservation for posterity. Political leadership addresses climate change mediating discussions on a fair share of the global commons in the long run. Open discussions will advance mechanisms for a just common goods distribution in the international interest.

On the political level, the correct price for fossil fuels must be found to offsets CO_2 damages. Based on estimates of the costs of climate change – such as, for instance, the Stern Review (2006) report – climate change agreements should target at implementing a world market price to avert climate change through CO_2 emissions taxation. Prices not only have a signal function but are also moral nudges. Letting corporations pay more than the harm caused by their consumption, creates governmental revenue to offset the downsides of climate change. If the tax is high enough, it becomes socially responsible if corporations use energy as for paying for the negative downsides of energy consumption. Taxation also alleviates from a moral responsibility of making cognitively complex, ethical choices. Thereby taxation frees moral capacities to solve additional predicaments. Countries with higher taxation grant their populace more cognitive capacities to ease the burden of ethical decision-making, who are freer to tackle novel ethicality predicaments and thus ahead of territories without energy pricing systems. Pricing energy consumption can, therefore, avert climate change, create governmental revenues, serve as a moral guide and ethical capacity enhancing strategy.

The humanitarian dimension of climate change has to become central. Climate negotiations, UN Framework discussions, and UN agencies must address the impact of climate change on the most vulnerable who have done the least to cause climate change but who are affected most severely. Climate justice links human rights and development to safeguard those who carry a disproportionally large burden of climate change and amplifies the voices of future world inhabitants to ensure fairness to future unborn. Low carbon growth and access to energy for all using non-fossil fuel sources will ensure sustainable development. Developing countries must build resilience to the effects of climate change. Global partnerships and international alliances lead regarding the human rights of climate change aversion. Sustainable welfare education bestows with long-term foci to foresightedly strive towards climate justice for the sake of eternal equity. Philosophically intergenerational equity must become a moral obligation when considering the consequences of climate justice.

While international actors craft international laws on intergenerational equity, nation states implement intergenerational fairness by finding access to affordable renewable energy in innovative ways of new technologies and green retrofits. Energy efficiency can also be created by infrastructure changes of public transportation to reduce energy consumption. City designs can make streets more secure and arrange public transport for pedestrians. Education can trigger fundamental change processes in individual lifestyles to become more consumption conscientious and energy efficient.

4. 1. Ethical decision-making under social uncertainty

Decision-making research has been revolutionized by prospect theory. In laboratory experiments, prospect theory captures human to code outcome perspectives as gains or losses relative to an individual reference point, by which decisions are anchored. Prospect theory's core finding that monetary losses loom larger than gains has been generalized in many domains, yet not been tested for social status changes. Social status striving has been subject to social sciences' research for a long time, but until today we have no clear picture of how social status prospects relative to an individual reference point may influence our decision-making and action. Understanding human cognition in the light of social status perspectives, however, could allow turning social status experiences into ethicality nudges. The perceived endowment through social status may drive social responsibility. Ethicality as a socially-appreciated, noble societal contribution offers the prospect of social status gains given the societal respect for altruism and pro-social acts. An Überethical filling of current legal gaps or outperforming legal regulations grant additional social status elevation opportunities (Puaschunder, 2017c).

The following part provides an innovative application of social status theories in the sustainability domain. Building on prospect theory, two field observations of environmentally conscientious recycling behavior and sustainable energy consumption investigated if social status losses are more likely to be answered with ethicality than social status gains. Social status losses are found as significant drivers of socially-responsible environmental conscientiousness. Testing prospect theory for social status striving advances socio-economics and helps understanding the underlying mechanisms of social identity theories. Pegging social status to ethicality is an unprecedented approach to use social forces as a means for accomplishing positive societal change. Future studies may target at elucidating if ethicality in the wake of social status losses is more a cognitive, rational strategy or emotional compensation for feelings of unworthiness after social status drops.

Social status is as old as human beings. Already ancient sources attribute rights and allocate assets based on status (DiTella, Haisken-DeNew & MacCulloch, 2001). Status ranks individuals on socially valued individual characteristics and group membership (Ball & Eckel, 1996; Hong & Bohnet, 2004; Loch, Huberman & Stout, 2000; Ridgeway & Walker, 1995). At the same time, surprisingly scarce is the information on how individuals perceive status changes and how their social conscientiousness is related to social endowments. In general, social status upward prospects are seen as favorable – but the downside of social status losses is rather vaguely described and no stringent framework exists on how status prospects impact human decision-making and actions.

One of the most influential theories explaining human decision-making under uncertainty is prospect theory (Kahneman & Tversky, 1979). Prospect theory holds individuals' perceptions about prospective outcomes as individually evaluated changes from the status quo. Laboratory experiments find individual aggravation over losing monetary resources to be greater than the pleasure associated with gaining the same amount (Bazerman & Moore, 2008). Originally prospect theory was captured for monetary gains and losses but replicated in various fields (Levy, 1997). In the application of prospect theory, social comparisons have mildly been touched on – if we consider the impact social identities have on our day-to-day judgment, decision-making and actions (Loewenstein, Thompson & Bazerman, 1989). Understanding social status prospects' influence on individual behavior, however, could explain the underlying socio-psychological motives of decision-making in the social compound. More concretely, if certain social status prospects are found to be perceived as more or less favorable, they are prone to elicit certain behavior and may steer respective action. In individuals' constant striving for favorable social status enhancement, social status prospects could put people into a specific mindset that drives pro-social acts.

As a pro-social behavior, ethicality is socially honored. In the social compound, ethicality offers social status elevation prospects derived from respect for socially valued altruism. Ethicality as a noble act may thus grant social status elevating opportunities. In reverse, social status perspectives could be used to nudge people into pro-social behavior (Thaler & Sunstein, 2008). The theory of nudging was introduced by Thaler and Sunstein (2008) drawing from psychology and behavioral economics to defend libertarian paternalism and create a favorable choice architecture that helps people to fall for a more health choice intuitively. Classical examples how decisions can be influenced are anchoring, availability, representativeness, status quo and herd behavior to create environments that aid people making a choice that is beneficial in the long run and for the sake of common good. Applications of successful nudging range from food choice and health, over finance and retirement, to work discipline but also environmentalism.

Prospect theory holds status losses loom larger than status gains. Nudging theory provides innovative examples of how individual decision-making can be influenced subliminally by group memberships. Foremost social status losses may steer ethicality in the wish to regain social status based on a reference point relative to previously-held status positions. If ethicality is related to social status gain perspectives, social-status awareness could become a means to nurture a favorable climate within society. Social status endowments may thus be the core of socially responsible behavior; social status prospects the driver of the warm glow. In the light of ethicality being an implicit social status enhancement tool, social status losses are potentially answered by pro-social behavior. Social status manipulation could thereby serve as a non-monetary nudge to foster ethicality in society (Thaler & Sunstein, 2008). Prospect theory and nudging are proposed as means of social status enhancement with attention to regaining prior social status losses. Social status losses are portrayed to nudge people into pro-social action.

All cultures feature some form of social status displayed in commonly shared symbols. Social status attributions posit people in relation to each other in society (Huberman, Loch & Önçüler, 2004). As ascribed status can be improved throughout life, relative status positions are assigned in zero-sum games – thus one individual's status gain lowers another ones' status. Individuals implicitly weigh their social status based on the number of contestants in ranks above and below them (DiTella et al., 2001). In societal hierarchies, status is related to a diverse set of opportunities as different rules and availability of resources apply to variant social status positions (Young, 2011).

As an intrinsic fundamental human characteristic, people are concerned about their social status in relevant domains, leveraging social status striving into a pivotal motivation factor in human life (e.g., Coleman, 1990; Duesenberry, 1949; Friedman, 1953; Friedman & Savage, 1948; Mazur & Lamb, 1980; Ridgeway & Walker, 1995; Weber, 1978). Social status impacts on an individual's social identity and emotional state (Postlewaite, 1998). Status gains and superiority are associated with positive emotions and well-being derived from positive interaction (Bird, 2004; Galiani & Weinschelbaum, 2007; Hong & Bohnet, 2004). Individuals are psychologically satisfied when experiencing to be better off than others and feel uneasy when they see others doing better (Easterlin, 1974; Hopkins & Kornienko, 2004). Status losses are embarrassing and drive a desire to enhance one's self-image in the wake of experienced unhappiness and risk aversion (DiTella et al., 2001; Harbaugh, 2006).

In the social compound, we favor positive status superiority of our groups compared to groups we do not belong to (Tajfel, 1978; Tajfel & Turner, 1986). Favorable group membership experiences are based on social opportunities (Meeker & Weitzel-O'Neill, 1977; Ridgeway, Berger & Smith, 1985). Group members with high status have more control (Bales, 1951; Berger & Zelditch, 1985), receive more credit for success (Fan & Gruenfeld, 1998), and enjoy higher degrees of well-being (Adler, Epel, Castellazzo & Ickovics, 2000). In contrast, low-status group members are more likely to be neglected (Chance, 1967; Savin-Williams, 1979), more often blamed for failures (Weisband, Schneider & Connolly, 1995), and feel more negatively (Mazur, 1973; Tiedens, 2000).

Social status is directly related to social action and therefore provokes human behavior (Weber, 1946/2009). Social status may bestow agents with subjective meaningfulness. The individual may perceive himself or herself as part of the larger and may, therefore, plan actions to be socially favorable. Actions may also arise naturally and subconsciously (Thaler & Sunstein, 2008). The group has an anchoring guiding influence on the individual, which is described in very many domains ranging from sociology to history, politics, jurisprudence, ethics, and arts (Weber, 1946/2009).

The emotional, social and economic consequences of status striving and related decision-making appear as an open research question. Unsolved remains how social status pursuits drive motivation and behavior. No stringent decision-making pattern of social status prospects impacting on decision-making and human action can be given in the eye of social uncertainty. If social status endowments lead to more social conscientiousness or social status losses may loom larger than social endowment gains is an unsolved question. One of the most influential theories to predict human decision-making in the light of future uncertainty is prospect theory.

Prospect theory revolutionized decision-making sciences by capturing economic outcomes to be coded as gains or losses relative to a neutral reference point (Kahneman & Tversky, 1979; Schkade & Kahneman, 1998). In laboratory experiments, Kahneman and Tversky (1979) found individuals' perceptions about outcomes as evaluative changes from their current state. Based on deviations from the status quo, prospect theory depicts an S-shaped expected utility function for perceived monetary gains and losses with a convex value curve for gains and a concave value function for losses (Currim & Sarin, 1989; Thaler, 1999). A comparatively steeper loss than value function captures peoples' aggravation over losing money to be greater than their pleasure associated with acquiring the same amount of money (Kahneman & Tversky, 1979). Individuals taking losses more serious than gains are motivated to preserve their status quo (Bazerman & Moore, 2008). The status quo bias holds individuals to be risk averse in the domain of gains while they are risk-seeking when facing loss prospects (Jervis, 1992; Kahneman, Knetsch & Thaler, 1991; Kahneman & Tversky, 2000; McDermott, Fowler & Smirnov, 2008).

Overall, prospect theory has leveraged into one of the most influential social sciences paradigms (Kahneman & Tversky, 1992). In the manifold application of prospect theory, hardly any information exists on social status changes. Although social comparisons may directly affect decision-making under social uncertainty, decision-making in the eye of social status endowment prospect remains an underexplored scientific area. Until today, we have no information on the generalizability of monetary prospects on social status outcome perspectives and how decision-making is influenced by social status outlooks and endowments (Huberman et al., 2004).

While the idea that people care about their relative status is well-acknowledged in social sciences, the behavioral consequences of social status prospects are rather unknown (Güth & Tietz, 1990; Nowak & Sigmund 1998; Robson, 1992; Tooby & Cosmides, 1990; Wedekind, 1998). The applicability of prospect theory on social status perspectives is untested (Loewenstein et al., 1989). Already in the original presentation of prospect theory, Kahneman and Tversky (1979) envisioned applications onto more 'typical' situations of choice. Apart from prospective monetary outcomes, prospect theory was proposed to be investigated for probabilities, in which outcomes are not explicitly given and more likely to be based on skills and chances (Kahneman & Tversky, 1979). Especially the status quo bias being theoretically isolated from motivational and social factors raised questions about social references, future aspirations and recent gains and losses (Chernev, 2009; Levy, 1997, 2003; McDermott et al., 2008; Tversky & Kahneman, 1991).

First comparisons of monetary and social utility in relation to prospect theory were started by Loewenstein et al. (1989). The social utility was defined as the level of satisfaction derived from outcomes of the self in comparison to others that were depicted as an alternative or additional salient reference points. Regarding social comparisons and framing, Fox and Dayan (2004) found deviations from the original prospect theory in gain preferences over loss aversion.

Building on preliminary research that holds social status striving to lead to investors' risk aversion (Roussanov, 2009) and happiness being dependent on relative comparison results, Falkenstein (2006) argues that people become more risk-seeking when facing negative social comparison outcomes (Axelrod, 1984; Easterlin, 1974; Siegel, 2002). One application of prospect theory in social contexts showed that accommodations to losses tend to be slower than to gains and people incur excessive risks to recover from social status drops (Jervis, 1992; Levy, 1997). The view of social status striving as a driver of risk-seeking behavior is also supported by descriptive research on wealth distribution and entrepreneurship (Cole, Mailath & Postlewaite, 1992). Naturally following experimental extensions of prospect theory could integrate the role of social comparisons for judgment and decision-making – as outlined by Festinger's (1954) social comparison and Adams' (1965) equity theory.

As most of our decision-making takes place in social and hierarchical contexts, applying prospect theory for social reference dependence appears as an interesting and necessary extension. In an attempt to explain the underlying socio-psychological motives of human decision-making under social uncertainty, investigating prospect theory in the social status domain will help understanding the behavioral consequences of social status prospects. In addition, becoming knowledgeable about emotions and behavior consequences related to prospective status changes could help unraveling the bounds of collective decision-making and overcome harmful collective decision-making outcomes – such as risk shifts, social stratification and group polarization (Janis, 1982). Finding how social status perspectives drive our actions and steer emotions will also enable us to create certain social status experiences that may instigate pro-social behavior. In particular, social status prospects could be used to drive ethicality.

Social status comprises of individual characteristics but also the amalgamated social status ascribed to groups one belongs to. Social identity captures that the mere belonging to a group contributes to an individual's status and self-esteem derived from the assigned respect towards membership groups (Tajfel & Turner, 1979). As social identities are related to a certain social status, exposure to social identity cues create situations of heightened social status awareness that influence the self-esteem. Social identity experiences put people in a specific mindset that affects their self-worth and determine their decision-making and actions.

In an implicit social hierarchy of social groups, individuals are in a constant struggle for status by orienting themselves onto higher social status groups they aspire to enter (Sidanius & Pratto, 1999). Social group membership cues of groups with higher social status steer the wish to belonging to a group. The longing to gain access to higher social status groups and striving for their respect could enhance compliance on collectively shared goals.

Social status provides opportunities to distinguish among each other (Bourdieu, 1979/1984). Social status prospects translated to economic means motivate people's actions. Cultural capital, such as elite education may promote social mobility opportunities that satisfy a zest for social mobility improvement (Bourdieu, 1979/1984). Different social classes may be established through education that constitutes and cultivates a certain taste within society. Certain habits learned in educational institutions may be a foundation of different types of social classes (Bourdieu, 1979/1984). Education distinguishes social classes. A certain predisposition towards solving social situations may be acquired through education, which eventually leads towards class-based social groups handling social situations differently. Social choice preferences learned in educational institutions may be the foundation of social class differences. Predispositions to certain kinds of values – including the preference for ethicality – may be instilled in children through education, which creates a certain taste for social conscientiousness (Bourdieu, 1979/1984). The beauty of Ivy League education may be to enter a certain social class and impede upward social mobility, but also entail the positive externality to acquire social responsibility and taste for ethicality (Puaschunder, 2016c).

In these features, social identity experiences could be used to change peoples' actions according to social norms. In an implicit social contract, social norms trigger solidarity on common goals and cultivate virtues within society – foremost through emotional experiences. Groups bestow with self-worth elevating pride when members are complying with socially favorable goals and shame arises when individuals act socially irresponsible. Fear of social status losses breaks unfavorable anti-social habits. Through emotions, exposure to social identity and social norm cues may drive social responsibility. Emotions depending on social experiences could be used to drive pro-social action. Social forces could steer social norm compliance based on emotional experiences in the light of social status prospects. Pegging social identity to social norm cues may create a specific mindset that influences the judgment and decision-making of individuals who may then act in a socially favorable way. Through cognition and emotions, social status prospects and social norm cues may trigger social norm compliance contributing to ethicality.

Ethics capture social responsibility based on explicit and implicit social norms. Ethicality not only comprises people choosing not to do wrong or when people unconscientiously enter a slippery slope leading to unethicality (Bazerman & Chugh, 2005; Bazerman & Tenbrunsel, 2011; Tenbrunsel & Messick, 2004). Ethicality also depicts when human are outperforming legal requirements and policy recommendations in the search for doing more 'good' than required. In this natural human drive to do 'good' to others, humans are overdoing legal regulation whilst incurring costs and impose risks onto themselves. Similar to Zimbardo's heroic imagination (2011a,b) describing the voluntary service to others that involves a risk to physical comfort, social stature or quality of life; this kind of Überethicality captures the voluntarily filling of legal gaps or outperforming of public policy goals that impose costs and risks onto the individual. In closing current legal gaps, the evolutionary-based natural law of Überethicality is forerunning legal codifications if considering laws to be the expression of our shared nature and amalgamated sum of societal norms over time (Cicero in Keyes, 1966).

Ethicality offers potential implicit or explicit strategies to express and enhance social status in the social compound. In general, the natural behavioral drive of Überethicality ignites without material gain prospect. To draw an extreme example, Mother Theresa was monetarily unfortunate, yet obtained highest social status for her Überethical pro-social work. In addition, financial investors who gained a fortune by rational market calculus are often prone to feel they have to return to society by philanthropy – for instance, Warren Buffett and George Soros dedicate extraordinary amounts of time and money to promote ethical causes.

Apart from monetary considerations, Überethicality derives from social incentives in the social compound. Status may play a key role. Based on Maslow's (1943) hierarchy of needs, one can only be Überethical if having reached a certain social status. Not having to worry about food and shelter, frees mental capacities to address higher societal, ethical needs and future-oriented filling current legal gaps. As ethicality is perceived as a noble act that grants others' respect, individuals may use ethical decisions as a conspicuous social status symbol in the social compound. Beyond governmental regulation and legal obligations, the nobleness of Überethicality may bestow individuals with social status elevation prospects. The foresightedness of fulfilling future requirements also implies leadership advantages (Young, 2011). Given the natural respect for the voluntary willingness to incur risks for the sake of pro bono-outcomes as well as leadership advantages attributed to pro-actively tackling ethical problems that may likely cover future regulation, Überethicality is thus an implicit social status elevation means apart from any monetary gains.

Under the assumption of individual self-esteem being dependent on social status and human constantly wishing to maintain or gain positive social status, Überethicality is seen as a social status pedestal. How social status striving can drive socially responsible behavior will be studied in an elite education setting. Social preferences as a context-dependent phenomenon will be observed at an educational hub that individual enter with the hope to improve their social standing and cultural capital. Pro-active ethicality can be used to claim or regain social status. In accordance with prospect theory holding that losses loom larger than gains based on an individual reference point, especially the prospect of losing prior social status may trigger individuals' wish to compensate social status losses by gaining status through ethical acts. This phenomenon will be captured at points in life when young people are eager to enter a higher social class and acquire the social skills to successfully transfer to societal upper classes. The idea to use social status prospects as a means to elevate pro-social behavior is novel and an innovative nudge to drive social conscientiousness in the sustainability domain (Thaler & Sunstein, 2008).

In order to reveal whether social status is related to ethicality in a way prospect theory would suggest; two studies investigated if social status prospects lead to a rise in ethicality and if – in accordance with prospect theory and Überethicality assumptions – social status losses are associated with higher degrees of ethicality than social status gain prospects at an elite educational institution.

In accordance with prospect theory and Überethicality notions, study 1 tested if social status losses are more likely to be answered with ethicality than social status gain perspectives. People were nudged into ethicality in the prospect of losing social reputation and access to social capital in the educational sector and sustainability domain.

A field experiment was staged at dormitories of a North American elite university during the 2011 summer that scrutinized if (1) the mere presence of social identity in combination with social norm cues leads to a rise in ethicality; if (2) social status losses heighten ethicality more than social status gain prospects.

The empirical evidence collected in a university environment was chosen for the unique setting of young individuals joining the summer school eager to enter a higher social class and acquire the social skills to successfully transfer to a better social standing. Academic circles and university settings are opinion leaders and educators of future leaders and can, therefore, be considered as a valid social laboratory. The data collected itself was in the sustainability domain featuring application in recycling and energy light consumption with widespread applicability to very many different public and private sector social causes.

Four dormitories were chosen to stage field experiments featuring an observation of the summer school students' recycling behavior. Four similar on-campus summer school residences were selected for creating different status experiences. During a summer school at a North American university campus, the summer school students, comprising of high school students, lived in the regular university campus dormitories. In total 711 summer school dormitory-residing students' recycling choices were observed in 4 different dormitories. The female and male students – mostly from the United States – were summer school attendees, mostly in their last year of high school, who took 7-week long program to specialize in classes in the fields of 'Arts, humanities & social sciences,' 'Business,' 'Computer science, math, and engineering,' 'Foreign language & literatures,' 'Sciences,' and 'Writing & Journalism.' The university chosen was an Ivy League, and therefore a certain distinct social status bias occurs.

Per dormitory, an average of 178 students' environmentally conscientious behavior was recorded every working day of the observation period. All dormitories were home to summer school students with approximately the same schedule – for instance, summer school students faced the same arrival period, study and exam periods and move-out times. Extraneous influences that potentially could lead to a higher amount of disposals – like cardboard boxes from moving in or out were therefore assumed to be constant for all dormitories.

In order to capture the effect of social identity pegged to social norm cues on socially responsible environmental ethicality (Hypothesis 1), the impact of a three-week exposure to university logos and 'Sustainability' initiative logos on summer school students' recycling behavior was observed.

For six weeks during the 2011 summer school, the residing summer school students faced different environments. Some of them were exposed to logos of the University (Test condition 1 representing social identity status striving), others to 'Sustainability' initiative logos of the University (Test condition 2 representing social, ethical norms), others to both logos concurrently (Test condition 3 representing social identity status striving pegged to social, ethical norms) and even others did not see university logos or 'Sustainability' logos of the University in dormitory recycling areas at all (Control condition 1: neutral).

Four posters were placed in each of the selected test dormitories around the recycling bins and buckets. Two of the 8.3 x 11.7 inches sized poster displayed the university logo featuring the emblem and letters of the university slogan on a red shield and below the university name on a white bandage. Two other posters exhibited the 'Sustainability' initiative logo featuring the described emblem and letters of the slogan next to a green shield and on the right-hand side the words 'Sustainability' and the name of the university. Both logos were printed in color on individual posters filling approximately 2/3 of the poster. All hardcover print-outs of the university logo or 'Sustainability' initiative logos were secured by a waterproof, lucent shield. The posters were placed on the wall next to recycling bins and buckets with easily removable tape. A similar poster location in all dormitory recycling areas was chosen. No posters were placed on doors, fences, entry posts, gates, poles, utility or sidewalks.

In the test dormitory, four copies of the university logo or 'Sustainability' logos per dormitory were installed concurrently around the recycling bins and buckets. In order to have comparison groups, the recycling behavior in three other, independent university dormitories of a North American campus was observed during the entire six-week observatory period. In two of the other test dormitories, four copies of the university logo or 'Sustainability' initiative logos were placed around the recycling bins and buckets. The control dormitory remained without logo installment. The time of the logo exposure was balanced between dormitories – one dormitory remained without any logos in the first three weeks, and two featured no logos in the last three weeks in order to control for general temporal biases.

In the first three weeks, 153 students of test dormitory 1 were exposed to university and 'Sustainability' logos. Test dormitory 2, which hosted 161 summer school students, did not feature any logo exposure prior to a planned future 'Sustainability' logo exposure. Test dormitory 3 exposed university logos to 147 students. The control dormitory, in which 250 summer school students lived, had no logos.

At the beginning of week four of the field observation, the conditions changed for all the test dormitories. The 153 students of the test dormitory 1, in which students were exposed to university and 'Sustainability' logos, faced an environment without any logo exposure. The test dormitory 2, hosting 161 summer school students – that did not feature any logo before – now showed 'Sustainability' logos. In test dormitory 3 – with prior university logos exposed to 147 students – the logos were removed. The control dormitory, in which 250 summer school students lived, remained without logo exposure.

The recycling behavior of 2011 North American dormitories' residents was observed by recycled weighting disposals. Recycled waste was measured every day during the regular disposal collection in the four respective dormitories during the summer school. The recycled disposals were weighted on a regular scale. The weight of different recycling buckets was recorded manually on a paper spreadsheet and the data transferred onto an Excel computer spreadsheet later each day of the data collection.

The recycling behavior during times of exposure versus non-exposure to logos was compared within the test dormitory. In addition, the effect of logo-installment versus non-logo-exposure was captured between dormitories. The effect is determined by a significant change in the recycled disposals' weight.

The combined presence of university logos and 'Sustainability' initiative logos heightened common goals compliance. After a time of exposure to the combined logos, in the phase of the removed social status and social norm insignia, pro-social behavior increased significantly ($t_{(27)}=-2.042$; $p<.032$), which was not the case in any of the other dormitories. Figure 7 holds the recycled weight during university and 'Sustainability' logo exposure monitored within the test dormitory over time. Logo versus non-logo exposure impacts on recycled disposals' weight within the test dormitory. Removed university in combination with 'Sustainability' logos heighten recycling compliance significantly.

Figure 7: Within test dormitory comparison of recycled weight during university and 'Sustainability' logo exposure and afterwards

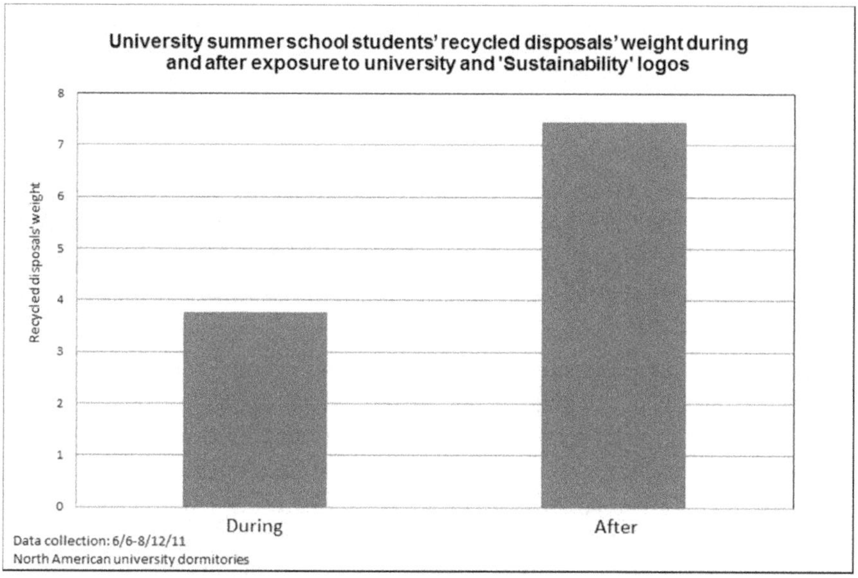

Figure 8: Between test dormitory comparison of recycled weight during university and 'Sustainability' logo exposure and afterwards

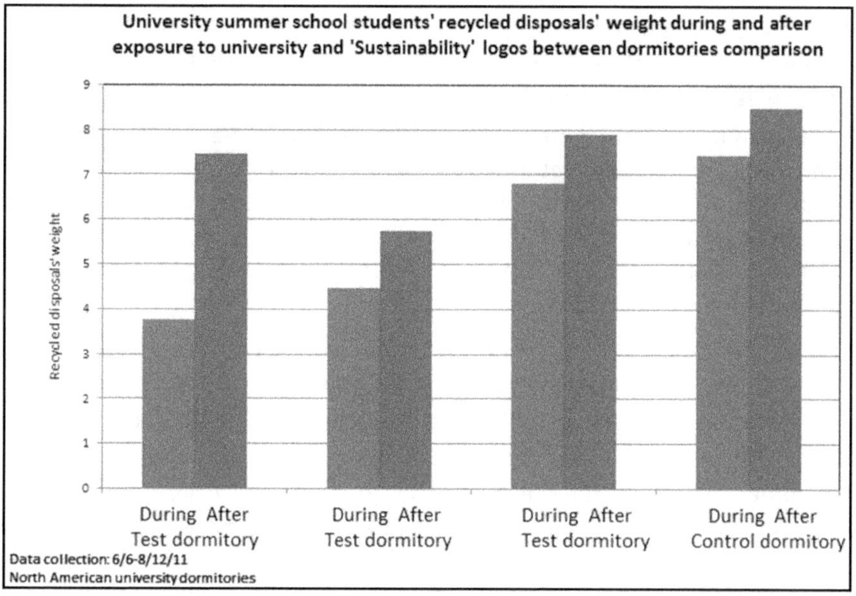

Figure 8 holds the recycled weight during university and 'Sustainability' logo exposure monitored within the test dormitory over time. Logo versus non-logo exposure impact on recycled disposals' weight within the test dormitory. Removed university in combination with 'Sustainability' logos heighten recycling compliance significantly.

Logo versus non-logo exposure impact on the environmental ethicality measured by recycled disposals' weight between the test dormitories and the control dormitory. Removed university in combination with 'Sustainability' logos heighten recycling compliance significantly when comparing between dormitories (One way ANOVA $F_{(7,104)}=5.914$, $p<.000$). Recycling compliance was measured based on the recycled weight per resident during exposure and after exposure to cues.

Study 1 provides evidence for ethicality being a context-dependent phenomenon nudgeable by social forces. Social status prospects can steer ethicality. Social identity and social status striving in combination with social norms can be used to improve day-to-day environmental protection behavior. Building on prospect theory, social status losses more likely trigger social norm compliance than prospective social status gains. Another study was designed to test if the effect of social status losses nudging people into social conscientiousness holds for environmentally conscientious energy consumption.

An additional field experiment at two North American university libraries targeted at investigating if (1) the mere presence of social identity in combination with social norm cues leads to a rise in ethicality and if (2) social status losses heighten ethicality more than social status gain perspectives.

The field experiment comprised of a field observation at two North American university libraries featuring user-controllable light-switches at reading desks and carrels. In a quasi-public location of two university libraries that are accessible by all general students, researchers and affiliates of the university, data was collected during six weeks. For six weeks, the energy light consumption was monitored and recorded manually.

In the first two weeks, the field experiment featured a baseline observation of energy light consumption without any installation followed by two weeks exposure to social status symbols and 'Sustainability' initiative logos featuring slogans followed by two weeks of removed logo exposure.

In order to capture the effect of social identity and social norm cues on socially responsible energy light consumption (Hypothesis 1) in a field observation, at one university library students were exposed to university logos (Test condition 1 representing social identity status striving) and

'Sustainability' (Test condition 2 representing social, ethical norms) at the respective university logos plus instructions to 'Please avoid losing energy by switching off lights after use' (Test condition 3 representing social identity status striving pegged to social, ethical norms) for two weeks. The postcard-sized (5.1 x 3.1 inches) stickers displayed the university logo and/or 'Sustainability' initiative banners stating 'Please avoid losing energy by switching off lights after use' in color filling approximately 2/3 of the card.

The cards were formed into cardboard tents. The tents were placed onto reading desks and carrels on three floors of one of the chosen university libraries. Per reading desk, either one or two tents were placed so that a person sitting at a carrel would see one tent. At the desks, three tents were installed so that approximately one to two people sitting down and using the reading desk would directly face one tent and could potentially also see two other tents. On the first floor of the test library, approximately 32 university logos were put on the reading desks and carrels. At the second floor of the test library, approximately 47 cardboard tents displaying the 'Sustainability' at the respective university logo were placed on reading desks and carrels under scrutiny so that one reading desk user could see one tent. On the third floor of the test library, approximately 120 cardboard tents displaying the university logo and the 'Sustainability' at the respective university logo were shown on the reading desks and carrels in similar locations per reading desk and carrel so that approximately one person could see one tent. All tents were maintained throughout the observation period and replaced on a daily basis if missing or damaged. As a control group, the energy light consumption of another library of the university campus was observed independently during the study. The control library (Control condition 1: neutral) remained without any logo or instruction placement.

The energy light consumption was observed several times daily in the respective libraries for six weeks. During the prospective observation time, the energy light consumption was recorded manually on a paper spreadsheet and transferred on an electronic computer spreadsheet on a daily basis. The library visitors were not informed about the energy light consumption measurement to avoid study participation biases. All information on energy light consumption was recorded in such a manner that the consumers were never identifiable insofar as linking the consumption to the individual library visitor, who were potentially university college and graduate students, postdoctoral researchers, scholars, and professors. All observation data was collected and analyzed anonymously. During the energy meter data collection, no contact with students or affiliates studying or working in the library was sought. At no point, there were any disruptive research activities that could influence or affect the study activities of library visitors.

The energy light consumption during times of exposure versus non-exposure to social status insignia and social norms instructions was compared over time within the test library and between the test and the control library. The recorded energy light consumption conscientiousness was measured by creating an index of abandoned burning lights divided by used burning lights per floor of the observed test library and the entire control library.

Figure 9: Between test and control library comparison of energy light consumption before and after logo exposure

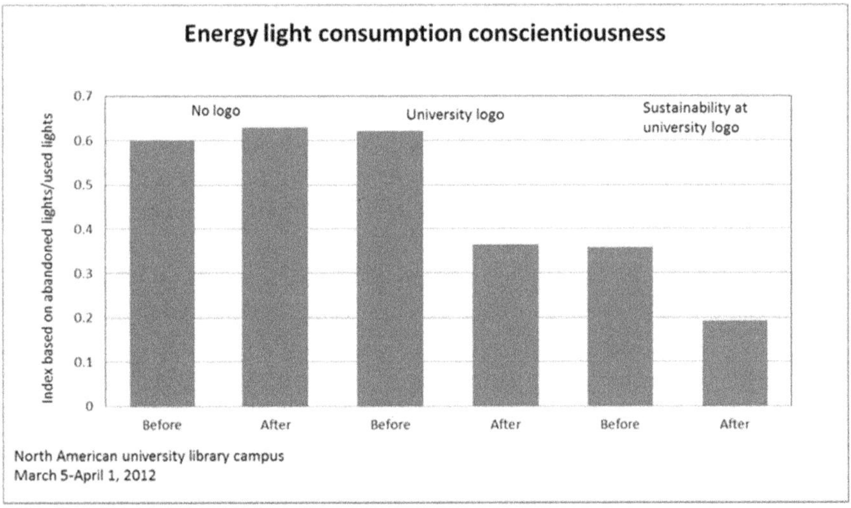

As Figure 9 exhibits, energy consumption conscientiousness significantly improved for the floors featuring the university logo (t=3.127, df=106, p<.002) for the two-week period after the logo had been removed. Improved energy consumption conscientiousness was found in the wake of removed university logos and social norm instructions. Energy consumption conscientiousness significantly improved for the floors featuring the 'Sustainability' at the university logo (t=2.898, df=85, p<.005) for the two-week period after the logo had been removed. When comparing the energy light consumption conscientiousness between the test library and the control library, there was a significant effect between libraries (ANOVA, F(3.578)=7.009, p<.000) after removed logos (p<.001). When comparing the test library floor featuring university logos and the control library, there was a significant increase of energy light consumption conscientiousness after the removal of status symbols in the test library (ANOVA, $F_{(7)}=6.695$, $p<.000$) after removed logos ($p<.025$). When comparing the test library floor featuring 'Sustainability' signs and slogans between the control library, there was a significant increase of energy light consumption conscientiousness after the removal of social norm cues and instructions in the test library (ANOVA, $F_{(7)}=6.695$, $p<.025$) after removed logos ($p<.000$). While there was a significant change in the light energy consumption in the test library, there was no significant change in the control library without any logos.

Overall, the presented studies provide evidence for ethicality being a context-dependent phenomenon. In the field of behavioral law and economics, connecting social status to ethicality contributes to the upcoming trend of sociology entering behavioral economics. Capturing social forces as the core of collective decision-making on social responsibility at the same time spearheads the idea of ethicality as a natural behavioral law. The presented results serve as evidence for situational cues as the driver of pro-social decision-making.

On a practical basis, pegging social status to ethicality is a novel idea to use social forces as a means for accomplishing positive societal change (Thaler & Sunstein, 2008). Unraveling social status striving affecting ethical decision-making thereby helps to foster socially responsible goals beyond stringent law enforcement and governmental policy control. Deriving information on circumstances under which decision makers are likely to exhibit social responsibility grants recommendations on how social forces can be used to stimulate socially responsible outcomes.

The presented connection of social status and social conscientiousness will help promoting ethicality. In a plethora of research on ethical downfalls and negative consequences of accidental ethical decision-making failures, Überethicality is a powerful contribution to strengthen our inner ethical forces. Understanding ethical decision-making under social uncertainty allows fostering a moral dimension of social life. Exploring further how psychological ownership and social status attributions can drive socially conscientious behavior offers cost-effective, easily implementable ethicality nudges to steer and promote socially responsible acts on a daily basis (Thaler & Sunstein, 2008).

The current research also serves as a way to better understand the socio-dynamics of environmental ethicality. The application of social identity on environmental ethicality is an unprecedented approach to prepare for major challenges ahead for humankind in the light of climate change and natural resources constraints. Finding circumstances under which decision makers are environmentally conscientious and potentially identifying social forces that trigger environmental ethicality is aimed at modeling day-to-day environmental protection decision-making and find easily-to-manipulate, real-world relevant sustainability incentives. On a grand scale, relating individual experiences to future common goals will allow public policy specialists designing context that advance the societal welfare and sustainable prosperity. Modeling the full realm of social decision-making promises nudges to steer civic virtues and motivate citizens to contribute to common goals.

Exploring ethicality in the light of social status drops is novel. The results lead to very many different applications in the public and private sector domains. The results can be considered transferable to other situations and social environments. For instance, even during the time when the paper was not published, it evoked research on social status losses as drivers of ethicality in the corporate domain. Age variant differences in social group membership relevance could be additional research areas evolving out of these preliminary results. The findings could also be transferred into other social domains, such as community service, ethical consumption, and charity giving. All these extensions would help solidify the case of a connection between social status and ethicality as well as social responsibility arising out of social status loss experiences.

As for future research, we do not have any further information whether this effect is more likely to be driven by a rational calculus or rather an emotional whim. Although we find social status losses to be answered with ethicality, we do not know if ethicality spikes in the eye of social status losses are caused by a more future-oriented rational calculus or more likely to be elicited by an unconscious wish to release from a feeling of unworthiness in order to compensate for unpleasant past social status losses. Unanswered remains in this finding whether social status related ethicality derives from a future-oriented cognitive strategy or a more subconscious emotional compensation mechanism in the aftermath of social status drops. Ethicality in the light of social status losses could be a rational calculus to gain a competitive advantage. In the wake of social status losses, individuals may strategically use pro-social acts to enhance their status by egoistic altruism (Becker, 1976). At the same time, social status losses could also be accompanied by feelings of unworthiness and ethicality be a means to compensate for hurtful losses. As such, ethicality may serve as a way to relieve from a feeling of unworthiness in the wake of former social status drops.

Future follow-up studies may, therefore, investigate if social status loss related ethicality is more likely to be associated with a rational profit maximization calculus or emotional loss compensation act. Exploring if social status-driven ethicality is more of a cognitive-rational strategy than subconscious, emotional, social status loss compensation will help to understand the underlying mechanisms of social identity and societal responsibility.

Future planned research could add laboratory experiments to back the findings in the field. Similar effects in a controlled environment, for instance by having students recycle under different conditions as they leave an experimental session or partake in some other type of ethical behavior, could back the hereby presented results. Extrapolating the results onto the organizational level would allow professionals to develop practical remedies on how to strengthen their inner moral muscle in a work setting. The distinct sample provides a peculiar snapshot of elite education, which leaves the generalizability of the results onto other religious groups, gender, age, and classes an open research question. On the micro level, it would also be interesting to see how the actual social environment plays a role and if the influence of social contexts changes throughout life. Additional research projects could address intercultural nuances of social status membership effects. Future investigations about different ethical dilemmas could provide additional practical applications of social status as a driver of ethicality following the greater goal of finding strategies how to ensure a pro-social and sustainable humankind.

4. 2. Joint decision-making in the public policy domain

In today's globalized world, the most pressing societal dilemmas require a focus on equity over time. Future-oriented intergenerational equity – or fairness in providing an equivalent standard of living to future generations – has gained widespread attention to ensure economic stability and sustainability (World Economic Forum, 2015). Intergenerational predicaments currently arise from unsustainable pension systems in the wake of an aging and shrinking Western world population, governmental overindebtedness in industrialized countries in the aftermath of the 2008/09 World Financial Crisis, as well as ecologic challenges in the light of climate change and unsustainable resource consumption. While future-oriented and socially responsible public policy-making has led to pressing challenges for public officials and policy makers, the legal background to ensure intergenerational fairness remains thin and policy implementations underexplored (Puaschunder & Schwarz, 2012).

In the public policy domain, decision makers are prone to be biased in their public choices (e.g., see Baron, 1998; Baron, Bazerman & Shonk, 2006; Stiglitz, 1998). In intergenerational choices, the implementation of future-oriented and socially responsible policies has been hindered by a lack of presence of future generations in voting situations, political lobbies, and current courtrooms. Decision-making biases were found to be exaggerated when choices are evaluated independently, such as being considered one-by-one (Milkman, Mazza, Shu, Tsay & Bazerman, 2012). A broad spectrum of decision-making alternatives presented concurrently has been proven to elicit more rational than emotionally biased choices (Milkman et al., 2012). Representing current and future perspectives together could thus help overcome a lack of familiarity with future conditions and bestow current decision makers with a future outlook. Future generations' living conditions are considered to be more salient in joint evaluations and brought to attention when being exhibited in contrast to current public policy choices. As the concurrent policy option, the presentation was found to improve the decision-making quality, imagining different generations' outcomes concurrently could help finding a well-balanced intergenerational equity equilibrium (Puaschunder & Schwarz, 2012). Comparing alternatives directly could aid decision makers when weighing costs and benefits over time and thus lead to more rational choices.

Testing the effect of two temporally distanced focused policies presented combinedly – a policy with focus now and another policy with focus later – is a novel attempt to curb harmful shortsightedness and offset psychological barriers to effective long-term choices. Bundling two policies into a single package could help making legislators more intergenerationally equitable in their decisions. To alleviate intertemporal decision-making fallibility by the joint representation of two temporal snapshots in time (now-and-later), however, has not been investigated yet.

When individuals judge alternatives, their decision-making is prone to be biased when evaluating alternatives one at a time. Contrary to standard utility theory would predict, presenting joint alternatives concurrently changes decision-making outcomes towards people becoming more rational (Bazerman & Moore, 2008; Gourville & Soman, 2005; Tversky & Shafir, 1992). A natural tendency towards evaluating choices jointly rather than separately improves the quality of decisions as it alleviates complexity and allows to trade-off alternatives directly (Bazerman, Loewenstein & White, 1992; Bazerman & Moore, 2008; Bazerman, Moore, Tenbrunsel, Wade-Benzoni & Blount, 1999; Bazerman, Schroth, Pradhan, Diekmann & Tenbrunsel, 1994; Irwin, Slovic, Lichtenstein & McClelland, 1993; Kahneman & Ritov, 1994). Decision-making failures can thus be curbed when several choices are presented together (Milkman et al., 2012).

When facing intertemporal dilemmas, presenting two generational points of view concurrently was therefore tested to be a useful tool to make the future present during the decision time. Especially in intergenerational predicaments, eliciting different generational viewpoints concurrently implicitly lead decision makers to make intergenerationally equitable choices. Joint decision-making thereby serves as a means to overcome intertemporal decision-making biases and in particular help implementing intergenerational equity in the public policy domain.

Two studies investigated the consequences of joint decision-making as potential intergenerational equity implementation strategy in the global public policy context. Extending the intertemporal choice literature and policy bundling strategies, the author and a colleague examined how presenting policies with the outcome now or in the future as singles or as combined bundles can bestow decision makers with a temporally widespread perspective. The concurrent presentation of two policy outcomes – one during an individual's lifetime and one beyond the lifetime – led to more intergenerationally equitable policy choices than the presentation of just the components of policies. The joint decision-making advantage's potential to nudge people into more temporally balanced choices was analyzed while paying attention to emotional, social responsibility components.

This joint decision-making advantage was also validated in an international context. The studies investigated if the policy advantage holds for a non-Western culture with differing intergenerational prospects than the Western world by samples from China (Study 1) and an international online collected data (Study 2).

Figure 10 summarizes Study 1 mean differences between single, combined and bundled presentation modes leading to significantly differing tax allocation preferences multiplied by the time of the policy impact index in the domains 'Education,' 'Foreign Aid,' 'Infrastructure,' and 'Environment.' All significant mean differences are indicated by brackets.

Figure 11 summarizes Study 2 mean differences between single, combined and bundled presentation modes leading to significantly differing tax allocation preferences multiplied by the time of the policy impact index in the domains 'Economics,' 'Education,' 'Foreign Aid,' 'Infrastructure,' and 'Environment.' All significant mean differences are indicated by brackets.

Figure 10: Study 1 joint decision-making advantage with different times of policy impact

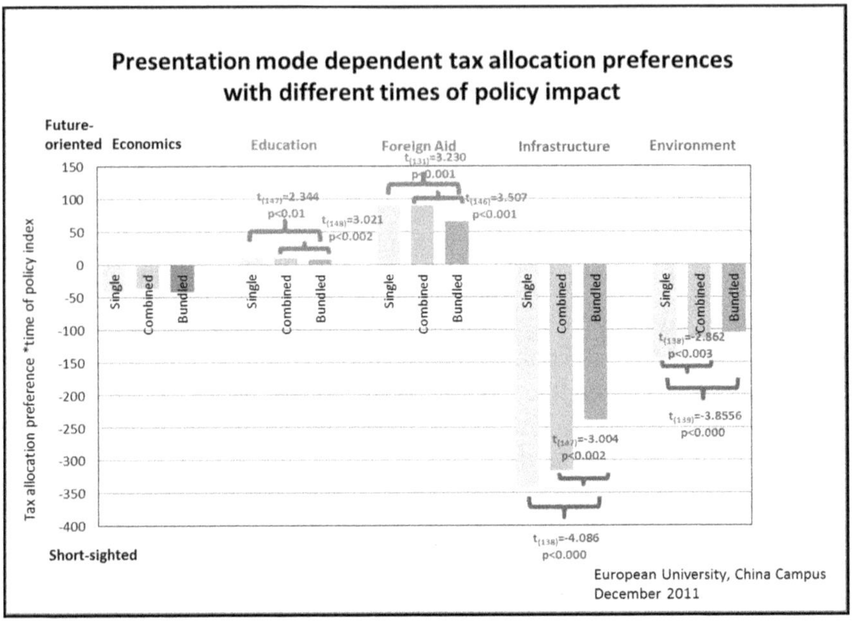

Figure 11: Study 2 joint decision-making advantage with different times of policy impact

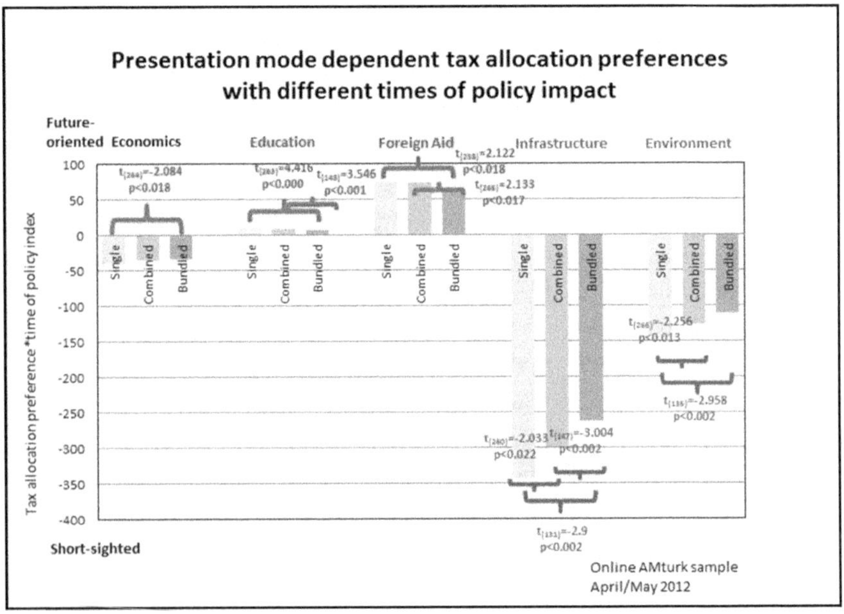

Both studies indicate that bundling policies with two different time snapshots and presenting policies with the outcome now and later in a combined manner led to more intergenerationally harmonious decision outcomes rather than when only one of their component pieces is present. This policy bundling strategy was found as an intergenerational equity implementation nudge. The combined presentation of public policies with the outcome now and in the future reduced the potentially harmful effects of focusing on the present rather than discounting for the future.

The joint decision-making advantage was tested on intertemporal predicaments in the intergenerational public policy domain. Presenting the viewpoints of two generations (young-old) or outcomes (now-later) concurrently worked towards intergenerationally equitable preferences in public policy choices. Comparing two snapshots in time together puts people into a temporal mindset that helps alleviate harmful intertemporal decision-making dilemmas. A temporally dual vision nudges decision makers into a more intergenerationally equitable outlook. The temporal policy bundling strategy serves as a powerful tool for implementing intergenerational equity in the global governance domain.

Overall, the presentation of public policies in a combined or bundled manner increases the propensity to make intertemporally balanced and thus intergenerationally fair distributions. However, in the intergenerational equity domain, emotional facets that lead towards a propensity to contribute to social responsibility policies, are reduced by the combined or bundled policy presentation mode for policies about education, foreign aid, infrastructure, and the environment.

The results account for the first introduction of joint decision-making in the intergenerational equity policy domain. Theoretically spearheading behavioral economics theory, the hyperbolic discounting bias was outlined to be alleviated by presenting two snapshots in time concurrently. Adding to heterodox economic thinking, the results indicate that joint decision-making can be used as an intergenerational equity nudge. Bundling policies representing a longer and shorter time spectrum offers a choice architecture that allows decision makers to overcome the pitfalls of harmful intergenerational equity constraints (Thaler & Sunstein, 2008). The bundling strategy as a simple, straightforward and easily implementable real-world policy-making tool can be used to aid legislators to consider future outcomes in their current decision-making. It may help public policy decision makers to overcome a short-term focus that can lead to long-term losses and irreversible environmental lock-ins infringing on future generations' standard of living. The policy bundling strategy was also found to work – according to our predictions – regardless of individual reference points. The studies demonstrate that the joint decision-making advantage holds throughout an international context. The robustness of the effect supports joint decision-making as a public policy tool in the global governance domain that can avert global common good problems. The results suggest that the policy-bundling method can guide legal scholars and policy practitioners to pass intergenerationally conscientious legislation. Connecting policy presentation forms to future common goals reveals pinpointing circumstances under which policy technocrats and political decision makers are likely to adopt intergenerationally conscientious solutions. This may lead them closer to pursuing the greater goal of temporal justice and thereby ensure a sustainable humankind.

4. 3. Trust and reciprocity drive social common goods contribution norms

One of the most prominent forms to create revenues for public causes are taxes. Taxation is codified in all major societies and a hallmark of democracy. Aimed at redistributing assets to provide public goods and ensuring societal harmony, taxation improves societal welfare and breeds social harmony within society.

Tax compliance is a universal phenomenon based on cooperation in the wish for improving the social compound. Taxpayers voluntarily decide to what extent to pay or avoid tax that limit the personal freedom – if considering the departing with personal funds for the sake of contributing to common causes. In a social dilemma, individual interests are in conflict with collective goals. From a myopic economic perspective, the optimal strategy of rational individuals would be not to cooperate and thus evade tax. Short-term the single civilian tax contribution does not make a significant difference in the overall maintenance of public goods – if only a few taxpayers evade taxes, public goods will not disappear or be reduced. However, if a considerable number of taxpayers do not contribute to tax over time, common goods are not guaranteed, and ultimately everyone will suffer from suboptimal societal conditions.

Contemporary economic research has focused on costs and risks of tax evasion. Coercive means – such as audits and fines – were found to crowd out tax morale and result in greater non-compliance as people feel controlled and not trusted. In the last decade, researchers have started to recognize the importance of incorporating morals and social dynamics in economic theory on tax behavior.

When analyzing tax behavior, recently behavioral economics insights have drawn attention to social influences. Tax psychologists widen the lens for a socio-psychological understanding of tax compliance. Social dilemmas have been replicated in laboratory settings that capture participants' decisions to cooperate or defect on common goods pools in order to derive realistic models of tax compliance.

Most recently, social nudge theories apply behavioral economics insights to change people's tax behavior. Apart from governmental control and sanction mechanisms, social situations were found to determine tax cooperation. Social setting directly influences tax compliance. In social dilemma experiments, participants' cooperation increases if their behavior is publicly known if they are allowed to communicate with each other, and mutual sympathy is established. As the antecedents of social tax, ethical norms and situational cues to elicit tax compliance are yet unknown. The role of the perception of fairness in the allocation of taxes within society for tax compliance remains an open research question in the emerging field of tax psychology.

From the psychological perspective, individuals are altruistic, but human comparisons with each other may play an essential yet unexplored role for tax compliance. Fairness regarding tax burdens could be positive drivers of tax compliance. A just perception in the allocation of common tax burdens could aid in overcoming the associations of individual losses in the 'burden of taxes.'

Voluntary, self-chosen tax ethics influenced by situational cues have just recently been covered by behavioral approaches towards public administration. In general, social norms define internalized standards how to behave. Internalized social norms are based on comparisons with one-another that may determine tax morale. Social norms elicit concurring behavior when taxpayers identify with the goals of a group but also if they feel being treated in a fair way within that group. Social fairness considerations in a tax reference group may thus be essential for taxpayer compliance. Fairness is believed to decrease egoistic utility maximization. Social perceptions of fairness underlying social norms are therefore potential tax ethics nudges. Tax morale may only emerge if individuals compare themselves with other groups and feel that the tax burden is distributed in a fair and just manner. Taxation non-compliance may stem from the notion of unfairness in how the tax burden is weighted heavier on some parts of society. But these psychological facets of fairness in the formation of social norms have been left out of economic calculus.

How to breed a perception of fairness in taxation throughout society? Fairness in tax perceptions may stem from the feeling of being treated in a respectful way by the government. People tend to adhere to a social contract in the relationship with their government. According to this psychological bonding with the community and well-perceived relation to the government, taxpayers feel a self-imposed obligation and willingness to comply with tax requirements if governmental actions are favorable to ensure tax compliance.

In a tit-for-tat strategy, taxpayers' compliance may depend on public goods provided by the government but also on the procedural and distribute justice perceived within society. Based on the interaction between tax authorities and taxpayers, taxpayers see themselves as members of a social group, whose social norms to follow fills them with pride and to whom to contribute feels right if being offered a fair deal. Convincing the public that taxation is fair and leads to a public good appears to require a multi-dimensional conception of taxes as a dynamic social phenomenon, which currently does not exist.

While the importance of societal norms for tax compliance has been studied, the role of the perception of fairness during the social comparison process and social norm learning to follow taxation rules has been overlooked. Research on tax compliance has focused on personal ethics and subjective perceptions of behavioral habits in taxpayers' reference group. Innovative tax psychology studies refer to social situations breeding tax ethics. Citizens' approval of tax politics is hypothesized to depend on fairness notions and cooperation between citizens and the community.

Tax evasion has negative effects on the national budget and suboptimal consequences for the general populace. The post-2008/09 world financial crisis era being characterized by governmental bailouts leverages tax compliance into a pressing issue of concern. In times of overindebtedness, tax fraud bearing unfavorable societal costs has reached the need for taxpayers' compliance to unprecedented necessity.

Understanding the socio-dynamics of tax ethicality follows the greater goal of finding strategies how to steer a pro-social society. Deriving information on circumstances under which decision makers are likely to deviate from rational profit maximization in common goods allocations helps modeling individual tax ethics. Elucidating the role of social forces in economic tax allocation decisions opens ways to imbue a civic tax ethics virtue based on a cooperative relationship within society. Finding tax ethics nudges provides strategies to elicit taxpayers' voluntary compliance. Identifying tax ethics triggers is aimed at modeling day-to-day societal decision-making. Based on the findings, institutional technocrats are enabled to design social contexts that automatically raise social conscientiousness and help implementing institutional models that motivate citizens to contribute to common goals.

The administration of the tax system is monetarily costly and raise questions how to control the controllers and make taxpayers follow the law. If taxpayers trust the government and tax authorities, the tax climate is likely favorable. Taxpayers base their trust on the experiences with tax authorities. Outlining the importance of trust and fairness for collective decision-making is an innovative attempt to help policy makers improve tax ethicality in the absence of law enforcement and governmental control (Ostrom, 2009).

Determining trust and reciprocity as the basis of socially favorable tax allocation outcomes helps government officials to reach common goals and establish justice. Overall, outlining the role of trust and reciprocity as means to implement tax compliance fosters the greater goal of ensuring a sustainable and fair society.

In the emergent field of tax psychology, the focus on regulating tax evasion recently shifted towards searching for situational cues that elicit common goals compliance. Trust and reciprocity are argued to steer a socially favorable environment that supports social tax ethics norms. Experiments that were staged, in which 256 participants played an economic trust game followed by a common goods game, found evidence for trust and reciprocity leading to individuals contributing to common goals (Puaschunder, 2015e). The more trust and reciprocity was practiced and experienced, the more common goals were supported – leveraging trust and reciprocity as interesting tax compliance antecedents. The results have widespread implications for governmental-citizen relations. Policy makers and public servants are advised to establish a client relationship with citizens breeding trust and reciprocity in order to reach common societal goals.

The findings of an experiment outline trust and reciprocity experiences driving common goods allocation preferences. In order to derive information on concrete drivers of the mechanism, future-oriented and socially responsible decision-making was also recorded. The results of two ranking tasks vary leading to the conclusion that common goods allocation preferences may be determined by the interplay of trust and reciprocity. The presented relation of trust, fairness, and reciprocity driving social common goods contribution norms offers practical recommendations for tax authorities. Unraveling ethicality triggers in trust and reciprocity breeding social tax compliance norms holds implications for institutional market communication and governmental information campaigns. Connecting trust to common goals compliance allows policy technocrats and political decision makers to help citizens adopt societally conscientious solutions.

Finding evidence for the importance of the government-citizen relationship for tax compliance implies that tax authorities are advised to treat taxpayers respectfully. Rather than responding to tax non-compliance with intrusive audits and severe punishment, supportive communication and collective interaction inspiring trust and reciprocity promise to encourage tax compliance. Replacing hunters-cops-and-robber's strategies featuring control and sanctions for developing trust and reciprocity in a service-oriented tax ethics approach will help foster tax compliance within future societies.

New cultures of customer relations orientation can create a cooperative tax climate. A cooperative contractual relationship and psychological contract apart from control and punishment should feature respectful client-oriented interactions in order to build trust and improve fiscal conscientiousness (Kirchler, 2007). Tax authorities are advised to consider taxpayers as customers. A new culture of customer relationship orientation appears more promising in enhancing cooperation and voluntary compliance without governmental oversight. In a service and client approach, taxpayers and tax authorities should create a climate of mutual trust and reciprocity based on clear and understandable regulations, transparency of procedures as well as respect and politeness for citizens. Taxpayers are more likely to report honestly if they feel that they are being treated courteously by the tax agency. If tax authorities and officers treat taxpayers equally, in a respectful and responsible way, the trust in the institution and cooperation increases. Tax authorities should also communicate to enhance a feeling of civic duty. Community responsiveness and citizen communication will raise public good contribution norms as the landmark of national stability and societal wealth.

Regarding future directions, cooperative strategies of self-regulation and education will help gaining tax compliance. Trainings of tax officers and organizational improvement to offer effective advice and problem resolution will foster public relations resulting in enhanced tax compliance. Tax education and support of tax agents as clients will aid taxpayers to understand the necessity of contributing to common goals. Educating taxpayers to be cooperative citizens and service client atmospheres will lead to taxpayers' voluntarily compliance. Trust and reciprocity could also be enabled through positive rewards and raising awareness for social obligations. Fostering relations of trust and reciprocity will establish a psychological contract between government officials and citizens. Tax contributions in an atmosphere of mutual trust and reciprocity will further breed a positive tax morale and voluntary compliance (Feld & Frey, 2005; Frey, 2003; Tyler, 1990). Avenues for future research may consider procedural fairness as an additional driver of tax responsibility. Personal identification with friends, occupational groups or the nation could also be investigated as tax compliance moderators following the greater goal of enabling common goods for this generation and the following.

Chapter 5

Intergenerational Transfers

Globalization led to unprecedented intergenerational equity imbalances regarding climate change, overindebtedness in the aftermath of the 2008/09 World Financial Crisis as well as pension reform needs of an aging Western world population (Puaschunder, 2015d). In the eye of current intergenerational concerns, the study of global intergenerational balances leverages into a necessary and blatant demand but is up-to-date limited. Intertemporal transfers between generations have not been captured on a global scale. Pursuing to fill laissez-faire gaps on intergenerational concerns, outlining public or private sector endeavors in coordinating intergenerational exchange would provide concrete means how to balance intertemporal benefits and burdens between overlapping generations in a fair manner (Broome, 1999). In the extensive contemporary writing on inequality, unraveling intergenerational equity opens ways to steer intertemporal social mobility (Arrow et al., 1999; Becker & Tomes, 1986; Piketty, 2014; Puaschunder, 2015b).

Classical optimal growth theories (Solow, 1956; Swan, 1964) featuring a traditional focus on capital and labor as well as intertemporal optimization growth models (Cass & Yaari, 1967; Koopmans, 1965; Phelps, 1961, 1966; Samuelson, 1975 a, b; Shell, 1967; Tobin, 1967; von Weizsäcker, 1962) based on Ramsey's (1928) intertemporal optimization idea, must be extended for intergenerational transfers. Traditional intertemporal discount rates and weighting functions are demanded to be replaced with a more dynamic and humanistic approach to capture intergenerational transfers paying attention to the need of subjective time discounting and social conscientiousness. Building on behavioral decision sciences and humane natural 'principles of personal good' (Broome, 1991; Laibson, 1997); behavioral economics insights on intergenerational equity find social responsibility and future orientation as prerequisites of intergenerationally conscientious decision-making (Wade-Benzoni & Tost, 2009).

Contrary to traditional capital-labor input factor views and optimization discounting, proposed macroeconomic intergenerational transfer models could leverage the micro-behavioral variables of the two independent dimensions social responsibility and future orientation onto a macroeconomic niveau to constitute an intergenerational transfer in the *public* and *private* sectors. The intergenerational transfer will thereby be macroeconomically described as a function of social responsibility and future orientation:

$$i = f(s, o), \qquad \text{(Equation 5.1)}$$

whereby i represents intergenerational transfer, f is function, s denotes social responsibility, and o describes future orientation. In order to study intergenerational transfers whole-roundedly, economic, social and environmental intergenerational benefit and burden sharing were captured, which will be outlined in the following. As dependent variables, environmental, economic and social intergenerational transfers were investigated regarding public and private preservation of resources (benefits distribution) as well as responsibility for cost and/or deficit (burden sharing) among different generational classes.

Figure 12: Intergenerational transfers in economic, social and environmental domains

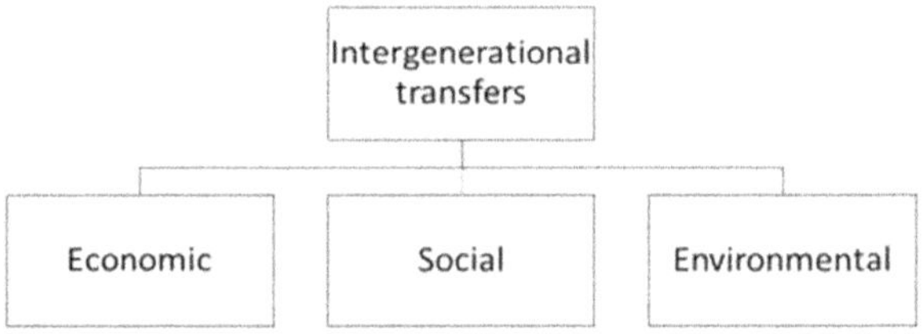

5.1 Economic transfers

The economic, social and environmental transfers were studied. Economic public intergenerational transfers were expressed in long-term infrastructure investment and maintenance as benefit preservation retrieved from the OECD International Transport Forum[1] as well as public deficit spending burden sharing.[2] Private economic intergenerational transfer is measured by inter-family wealth transfers benefits distribution estimated from inheritance

[1] https://stats.oecd.org/index.aspx?queryid=47797
[2] Calculated by the formula ((Revenues – Expenditures)/Revenues)*100

tax statistics retrieved from The Brookings Institution[3] and intergenerational labor inequality burden-sharing based on age-related youth unemployment gained from World Bank databases capturing unemployment of youth in percent of total labor force aged 15-24 years based on World Bank provided International Labor Organization (ILO) estimates.[4]

Economic public burden sharing was measured by public deficit spending. Information on national public budgets was retrieved from the Central Intelligence Agency (CIA) World Factbook.[5] The budget deficit information was then related to the overall budget by calculating a country's total revenues minus the country's total expenditures, divided by revenues and the overall term multiplied by 100. The equation of this procedure reads

$$\left(\frac{r_c - e_c}{r_c}\right) * 100, \qquad \text{(Equation 5.2)}$$

Whereby r_c represents total country revenues and e_c stands for total country expenditures.

Economic, public benefit transfer was retrieved from OECD long-term public infrastructure investment and maintenance spending data captured in the International Transport Forum chart on the investment in inland transport infrastructure as a percentage of GDP.[6] The most recent data, ranging from 2011 to 2005 was taken into consideration.

Economic *private* burden sharing was studied in youth unemployment as the share of the labor force aged 15-24 years without work but available for and seeking employment based on World Bank data compiling International Labor Organization (ILO) estimates for the years 2010-2014.[7]

Economic private benefit transfer was depicted by inter-family wealth transfers as outlined by the 2014 European Commission Cross-Country Review of Taxes on Wealth and Transfers on Wealth.[8]

The social public sector intergenerational transfers are operationalized by pay-as-you-go burden sharing public pension schemes and capital cover

---

[3] http://www.brookings.edu/views/papers/gale/20010126.pdf

[4] http://data.worldbank.org/indicator/SL.UEM.1524.ZS

[5] https://www.cia.gov/library/publications/the-world-factbook/

[6] https://stats.oecd.org/Index.aspx?DataSetCode=ITF_INV-MTN_DATA

[7] http://data.worldbank.org/indicator/SL.UEM.1524.ZS

[8] http://ec.europa.eu/taxation_customs/resources/documents/common/publications/studies/2014_eu_wealth_tax_project_finale_report.pdf

pension system benefit transfer is scrutinized in governmental public pension systems data of the OECD 2013 Factbook (OECD, 2013).[9] Private pension spending burden sharing and inter-family social benefits regarding household child care are described by the U.S. National Bureau of Economic Research and the OECD (Guryan, Hurst & Kearney, 2008; Veerle, 2011).[10]

Social responsibility was measured in the public sector by social capital estimates in the world using data from the World Database on Social Capital (García, Martínez & Radoselovics, 2008). Social capital refers to the collective value of social networks and the inclinations that arise from these networks to cooperate and enable collective action. Social capital encompasses institutions, relationships, and customs that shape the quality and quantity of society's social interactions.[11] As a critical prerequisite for societies to prosper economically and sustainably, social capital improves effectiveness and longevity of communities and their ability to work and function efficiently together. Social capital allows addressing common needs in the social compound fostering greater inclusion and cohesion as well as increased transparency and accountability. Social capital comprises of five key dimensions: (1) Groups and networks as collections of individuals that promote and protect personal relationships which improve welfare; (2) Trust and solidarity as elements of interpersonal behavior; (3) Collective action and cooperation as the ability of people to work together toward resolving communal issues; (4) Social cohesion and inclusion to mitigate risk of conflict and promote equitable access to benefits of development by enhancing participation of the marginalized as well as (5) Information and communication to improve social discourse and grant access to social knowledge.

For the private sector, the KPMG Survey of Corporate Responsibility Reporting 2013[12] served as an indicator of the social responsibility of the corporate world. Rates of corporate responsibility measured in percent of corporations reporting on social responsibility across 41 countries in 2013 were the basis for the independent variable private sector social responsibility (KPMG, 2013).[13]

---

[9] http://www.oecd-ilibrary.org/economics/oecd-factbook-2013_factbook-2013-en

[10] http://www.oecd.org/pensions/public-pensions/OECDPensionsAtAGlance2013.pdf

[11] http://web.worldbank.org/WBSITE/EXTERNAL/TOPICS/EXTSOCIALDEVELOPMENT/EXTTSOCIALCAPITAL/0,,contentMDK:20642703~menuPK:401023~pagePK:148956~piPK:216618~theSitePK:401015,00.html

[12] http://www.kpmg.com/Global/en/IssuesAndInsights/ArticlesPublications/corporate-responsibility/Documents/corporate-responsibility-reporting-survey-2013-v2.pdf

[13] http://www.kpmg.com/Global/en/IssuesAndInsights/ArticlesPublications/

Future orientation in the public sector was captured in governmental education investment spending based on OECD (2013) data of the Education at a Glance 2013 Report.[14]

In the private sector, future orientation was measured by the Culture and Leader Effectiveness GLOBE Study. The "Global Leadership and Organizational Behavior Effectiveness" (GLOBE) Research Program was conceived in 1991 by Robert J. House of the Wharton School of Business, University of Pennsylvania. In 2004, its first comprehensive volume on *"Culture, Leadership, and Organizations: The GLOBE Study of 62 Societies"* was published, based on results from about 17,300 middle managers from 951 organizations in the food processing, financial services, and telecommunications services industries. In 2007, a second major volume, "*Culture and Leadership Across the World: The GLOBE Book of In-Depth Studies of 25 Societies,*" complemented the findings from the first volume with in-country leadership literature analyses, interview data, focus group discussions, and formal analyses of printed media to provide in-depth descriptions of leadership theory and leader behavior in those 25 cultures. Today, the GLOBE study holds a unique set of cultural dimensions and culture clusters to capture leaders' effectiveness regarding the societal and organizational norms, values, and beliefs of the people being led. Within the GLOBE study, future orientation captures "the extent to which individuals engage in future-oriented behaviors such as delaying gratification, planning, and investing in the future" (House, Hanges, Javidan, Dorfman & Gupta, 2004, p. 282). Societies that have high future orientation feature characteristics such as propensity to save now for the future, emphasizing working for long-term success, organizations tend to be flexible and adaptive as well as view material success and spiritual fulfillment as an integrated whole.

Social public burden sharing was outlined by pay-as-you-go public pension system as well as benefit transfer from capital cover public pension systems retrieved from OECD databases of the OECD 2013 Factbook in combination with country information retrieved online, mainly from the European Commission.[15]

Social, private burden sharing was measured by private pension spending across countries as outlined in the databases of the OECD 2013 Factbook: Economic, Environmental and Social Statistics (2012).[16] Private benefit trans-

---

corporate-responsibility/Documents/corporate-responsibility-reporting-survey-2013-v2.pdf

[14] http://www.oecd.org/edu/eag2013%20(eng)--FINAL%2020%20June%202013.pdf

[15] http://www.oecd-ilibrary.org/economics/oecd-factbook-2013_factbook-2013-en

[16] http://www.google.com/url?sa=t&rct=j&q=&esrc=s&source=web&cd=1&ved=0CB4

fer in terms of household time spent on private child care was retrieved based on Veerle's (2011) OECD report as well as Guryan et al. (2008).

Environmental public burden sharing in intergenerational transfers were outlined in public prices in existing carbon pricing schemes provided in the World Bank 2014 States and Trends of Carbon Pricing Report.[17]

Public environmental benefit transfers were captured in the Inclusive Wealth Index,[18] which was jointly launched by the United Nations University's International Human Dimensions Programme on Global Environmental Change (UNU-IHDP) and the United Nations Environment Programme (UNEP). The indicator that was unveiled in the Inclusive Wealth Report 2012 (IWR), an initiative launched at the Rio+20 World Summit. The report looked at changes in inclusive wealth in 20 countries, which together account for almost three-quarters of global GDP, from 1990 to 2008 (Menchik, 1979).

Private environmental, intergenerational transfers feature household energy consumption benefit distribution based on electricity use per household. The average electricity consumption per electrified household in 2012 was measured by energy efficiency indicators of the World Energy Council.[19]

Private international waste management and recycling served as private environmental burden sharing indicator based on EUROSTAT data.[20]

The sample included per variable a maximum of 194 countries (Mean=55 countries; Median=36; Mode=33; SD=45.57; Minimum=8; Maximum=194 countries). In order to test for external validity, the variables were measured against similar variables between different data points from other external sources measuring similar concepts. In addition, internal validity checks were employed by calculating the correlations between the variables employed in the following regressions.

QFjAA&url=http%3A%2F%2Fwww.oecd-ilibrary.org%2Feconomics%2Foecd-factbook-2013_factbook-2013-en&ei=VQJLVd3xC4ykyATJhYDgBg&usg=AFQjCNEO0JAQ62KmwQ5zv182JfWJM9RsUA&sig2=EmvTrH5sTpv5FizAF8UaNg&bvm=bv.92765956,d.aWw

17 http://www-wds.worldbank.org/external/default/WDSContentServer/WDSP/IB/2014/05/27/000456286_20140527095323/Rendered/PDF/882840AR0Carbo040Box385232B00OUO090.pdf

18 http://www.unep.org/newscentre/default.aspx?DocumentID=2688&ArticleID=9174

19 http://www.wec-indicators.enerdata.eu/household-electricity-use.html

20 http://ec.europa.eu/eurostat/statistics-explained/index.php/Waste_generation_and_landfilling_indicators

Based on the results of regressions encompassing variables with up to 194 country data points, future-oriented parts of the world are characterized by environmental recycling and waste management conscientiousness, youth employment but also inter-family wealth transfer and less public pension care instead of public pension pay-as-you-go systems. Deficit spending countries are lower on social responsibility than those whose public leaders pursue a more balanced budget approach. CSR rate of corporate responsibility reporting is related to youth unemployment and public pension pay-as-you-go systems.

Analyzing data from 20 countries of the world, World Bank Social Capital estimates are negatively related to economic, public deficit spending based on CIA data. A cross-section regression holds a one unit change of social capital per capita index being related to a -.048 unit change in economic, governmental deficit spending. Therefore, the higher the level of social capital in a country, the lower the likelihood is of a government to engage in deficit spending and austerity policy-making. Innovatively outlining the relation of social capital and government debt is targeted at alleviating frictions arising from the up-to-date unknown negative socio-economic correlates of running governmental deficits heralding an unprecedented intergenerational equity kink. Potential overindebtedness remedies are reflected upon with a focus on the US and Europe in order to ensure a harmonious societal climate between generations.

While the study design may have its merits with capturing 194 countries in the first investigation of international differences in intergenerational macroeconomics, at the same time, the study design is bound by methodological limitations of a pilot study.

Future research could examine if interculturally-differing social responsibility and future orientation vary intergenerational transfers. Additional studies could address public and private sector contributions to intergenerational transfers but also capture if public sector social benefits are associated with the public intergenerational transfer and private sector contributions associated with the private intergenerational transfer. In addition, researchers could scrutinize if public and private sector intergenerational transfers are inversely related (crowding out) or can lead to complementary benefits. The intergenerational transfer model employs cross-section regressions and will include hierarchical linear modeling to outline between the continent and country differences in the following. Simultaneous equations models and value-added modeling are alternative tests to consider.

Based on the ideas of investments trumping consumption in intergenerational distribution calculus as well as compensatory gains and Pareto optimality of harmoniously concerted intergenerational transfers among the economic, social and environmental domains (Foley, 2009; Sachs,

2014) as well as behavioral economics findings of losses looming larger than gains (Kahneman & Tversky, 1979). Future research could target at differentiating between benefit and cost transfers from generation to generations capturing variance between intergenerational benefit transfer and intergenerational burden sharing in the triple bottom line domains.

As for methodological advancements, further investigations may employ econometric modeling in the realm of Bayesian statistics or model specifications and diagnostic tests as outlined in Gujarati and Porter (2009) and Hill, Griffiths and Lim (2012).

5. 2. Technological change

Technological progress is a formidable element for transformations at all levels of society. Technological change is therefore of pivotal relevance for the intergenerational transfer analysis. The following part introduces technological change as driving force for societal intergenerational equity considerations.

In the wake of globalization leading to an intricate set of interactive relationships between individuals, organizations, and states, technology innovations have caused an Information and Communication Technologies (ICT) revolution. Media innovations and ICT have become prominent with governments, the private sector, civil society, the new media community, and academia. In light of the growing importance of new media and social platforms role in instant communication but also education and crisis coordination, ICT is prospected to be playing a continuously rising role in sustainable development and guide intergenerational transfers (Puaschunder, 2017b).

New media and ICT enable reliable and accessible data to remain high on the agenda for governments, civil society, and other stakeholders. By engaging diverse actors and data sources, countries can better track progress, while deepening the ownership people and governments have of the results (SDGs Report 2016). The digital age is acknowledged to offer the potential to generate data that can inform government policies. The rapid growth of new technologies improves the possibilities to understand the world and expand communication across borders at an affordable price.

ICT can foster the greater goals of achieving international civil society progress, global crises prevention and societal deficiencies alleviation in cross-sectoral solution finding and policy dialogue on development. Within the civil society, social media innovations engage the greater public, NGOs, private foundations, and consumers. Scientific and academic ICT advocates, and also individuals and institutions provide oversight on information issues. Agencies implementing ICT programs for development contribute to intergenerational transfers (Puaschunder, 2017b).

ICT has recently become a vehicle for development-related issues as outlined in an as-such-themed advisory group to the UN Secretary-General (Puaschunder, 2017b). ICT enhances intercultural and cross-sectoral dialogues among stakeholders to globally address and facilitate the transfer of knowledge and societal progress. As an umbrella organization, the UN hosted GAID initiative (Global Alliance for ICT and Development) promotes the use of ICT for the achievement of the UN Sustainable Development Goals (SDGs) (World Economic Forum Report, 2015). The various GAID stakeholders contribute to advocacy and the policy debate on the role of the information society in international development. In a multi-stakeholder attempt, GAID facilitates PPPs to foster the dissemination of technological solutions for the achievement of development. As a networking governance platform, GAID steers the dissemination of innovations on ICT for development. The partners of the alliance have the overarching goal of tackling societal challenges in a knowledge-based information society. Partners demonstrate leadership on ICT and mainstream the global ICT agenda for the accomplishment of UN endeavors. Best practices knowledge on ICT is shared in policy dialogues and presentations of innovative business models for community investment, economic growth through access to new media technologies and the ICT empowerment of people living in poverty (Puaschunder, 2017b).

In recent decades, ICT revolutionized the availability and access to information. In the wake of the IT revolution, ICT has gained importance as a means of information dissemination in e-newsletters, blogs, and e-forums. As a multi-dimensional knowledge brokerage tool, ICT enhanced information synthesis and transparency. New media sources granted unprecedented accountability and benchmarking opportunities to stakeholders. Since the inception of GAID, the communication technology sector has been developing rapidly. The whole world, including economic actors, various national and international institutions and organizations as well as other stakeholders, have been trying to cope with the dynamics of instant communication transfers and technological reach around the globe. As of today ICT has strengthened global governance by improving the performance and efficiency of markets and governments and thereby directly contributed to society (Puaschunder, 2017b).

Regarding the UN SDGs, which were introduced in September 2015, ICT has become an important tool for the alleviation of societal deficiencies. As for the eradication of hunger, the IT revolution has perpetuated the efficiency in the information flow on drought, hunger, and crises. As an innovative avenue for fighting poverty, ICT provides access to capital online and by mobile phones. Information flow is key to the medical assistance for underserved communities and a pivotal prerequisite for effective epidemiology. As an essential feature of preventive medical assistance, ICT helps educating on maternal health and combating child mortality, HIV, malaria and other diseases. ICT has led to groundbreaking insights on the decay of natural resources and climate change. Technological change is of particularly high importance in the case of global warming. Information and communication foster environmental protection and sustainability (Puaschunder, 2017b).

Global technological revolutions will probably be related to energy. Therefore, implications for climate change for future generations have been analyzed in a framework with technological change and Gross Domestic Product (GDP) indicators. Contemporary Gross Domestic Product (GDP) measurements served as the basis for estimations about the productivity of the agriculture, industry and service sectors around the world in a changing temperature. The cardinal temperatures for the agriculture, industry and service sectors productivity, the average temperature per country around the world as well as climate projections of the year 2100 under the business as usual paths, reveal for the very first-time climate change winners and losers around the world (Puaschunder, forthcoming b). Human migration and Foreign Direct Investment (FDI) streams into the global warming winning countries are found (Puaschunder, 2017f). Overall and simply seen from a narrow-minded GDP perspective, the world will macroeconomically benefit more from climate change until 2100 than lose (Puaschunder, forthcoming c). This insight leads to the introduction of the climatorial imperative – advocating for the need for fairness in the distribution of the global warming benefits among nations based on Kant's categorical imperative to only engage in actions one wants to experience themselves being done to oneself (Puaschunder, 2017e). Passive neglect of action on climate mitigation is an active injustice to others. This research highlights the need for international global warming benefits transfers (Puaschunder, 2017e). While the method to measure the gains from climate change can certainly be refined in future studies, this research stream is meant as very first preliminary step to open a gate to legal codifications and policy work to settle for a right, just and fair distribution of benefits from our common warming mother earth (Puaschunder, 2017a). Focusing on gains may serve as means to hopefully draw attention to climate change of agnostic market actors or those who shy away from action given the overall negative connotation of climate change burden sharing and economic productivity loss aversion. Future research in this area should integrate technological advancements' impact on GDP.

In the intergenerational equity domain, new media technologies are pivotal to preventing environmental crises and managing risk in the domain of climate change. Access to information and the reduction of information transfer costs have helped educating underserved groups as an essential ingredient for societal development and the empowerment of minorities. Web-based communication has developed into an innovative teaching and learning method that features fast interactivity, cooperative learning arrangements and richness in content. As a communication and information tool for education, ICT is also key for minority advocacy and empowerment but lacking accessibility may cause problems in low-income countries. Within corporations, ICT develops competencies necessary for lifelong learning and employee empowerment. In the implementation of policies, ICT links minorities and local aid with global umbrella organizations. Overall, ICT strengthens policy-making bodies on a national and global level in collaboration with the UN. ICT fosters development progress throughout the world through instant communication opportunities and access to information (Reinfried, Schleicher & Rempfler, 2007).

Since the inception of GAID, changing technologies have been introduced in the age of digital big data revolution and information transition. Updated information on how the program has evolved helps draw conclusions about lessons learned. GAID has brought together many of the organizations previously central to ICT for development, such as the World Bank, the Swiss Agency for Development and Cooperation, the Global Knowledge Partnership (GKP), Canada's International Development Research Center (IDRC) and governmental stakeholders (ICT4D Report, 2009). Embracing partners from the private sector, global governance institutions, national governments, civil society organizations and research institutions, may have blurred the focus of the initiative (Puaschunder, 2017b).

The SDGs Report 2016 distributed at the 2016 International Conference on Sustainable Development hosted by Columbia University and The New School New York highlighted ICT playing a key role in the SDG implementation. The technology revolution enabled innovative and cost-effective methods based on mobile phones, mapping, sensors and satellite imagery to collect and improve data for development. But the use of these advances was found to require "new partnerships and collaboration between companies, institutions and civil society" (p. 14).

The SDGs Report 2016 also addresses the major challenge of the paucity of data and the poor information on groundwork systems that make it difficult to monitor and assess the implementation of networking systems. There needs to be a routine of follow-ups about the functioning of programs and a vital data collection and analysis over time to ensure the sustainability of long-term ICT for development strategies. Due to the variety of contexts, a good investment in information collection and processing requires a broad approach covering all contextual and economic factors relevant to universal ICT for development utilization. Incomplete essential information in the past has hampered development (Puaschunder, 2017b).

Today's decision makers have a more diverse array of facts easily available at hand. Yet for many of the poorest countries in the world this luxury remains inaccessible. As the SDG Report indicates, huge data gaps persist. The data deficit is partly a consequence of the lack of resources, especially when governments are struggling with inadequate budgets to invest in the latest data technologies. Data costs money, time and human effort to collect, which may be scarce, especially in the developing world. Nevertheless, investments in data collection pay off as information is invaluable for governmental executives for their decision-making in the allocation of scarce resources.

New media and ICT allow cross-sectoral solution-finding for intergenerational predicaments and long-term storage of information. Big data revolutions allow most sophisticated unprecedented policy dialog within overlapping generations. GAID introduced ICT for development in the international dialogue. In the future, international organizations and UN-related public-private-partnership networks should continue advocating for ICT for development on a global basis. Given the information retrieved online and from stakeholder reports, public and private actors engaged in advocacy and policy dialogue, corporate social entrepreneurship and philanthropy on ICT for development.

Making resources available for the poorest countries would be key in improving data systems. Donors and other partners play an essential role. According to the Sustainable Development Report 2016, making the most of the new opportunities presented by technology to make data faster, more accurate and more useful will take more than money. It will mean governments, researchers, the private sector, NGOs, and multilaterals working together to see how new data can solve old problems. Improving data collection and shared access to data thus needs to become a collective effort. New data at the same time will raise questions about privacy protection and with whom to share information (Puaschunder, 2017d). Public and private sector institutions will have to come together on a larger scale to provide, use and streamline information flows. The Sustainable Development Report advocates for further partnerships bringing together governments, companies, NGOs, UN-agencies and other multilaterals determined to improve production and increase the use of data to address sustainable development.

In the future, new media's assets to support existing intergenerational transfers and overlapping generations' networks should be investigated as well as ICT's value of embracing new stakeholders. Novel ICT initiatives that developed under UN guidance should advance the use of ICT for development on the regional, national and international levels. Data conservation to streamline actions for the advancement of common endeavors should be arranged in order to find an intergenerationally harmonious solution. ICT for overlapping generations use will allow having a track-record stronger emphasis on long-term goals. Endeavors pursuit could connect ICT to accomplishing the SDGs and the UN Global Compact goals. In this GAID and ICT would pay a broader value for intergenerational equity implementation efforts around the world.

Increasing the visibility of future generations in new media sources could aid to convey the idea of intergenerational equity. Providing access to information on future living conditions based on big data extrapolations by the use of computational innovations but also new media tools – e.g., e- newsletters, blogs, and Facebook – to foster engagement of a broad audience for future living conditions will improve access to information about intergenerational concerns. Internet information portals need to position ICT as a network hub for information exchange that attracts stakeholders' attention and raises the participants' commitment to contribute to this generation and the following's common goals.

In terms of stakeholder management, technology should play an active role in the coordination of different generational representatives' endeavors and fortify the intergenerational glue. Stakeholder engagement activities could bring together executives from international organizations and corporations, government officials, and the civil society to discuss ICT for intergenerational equity. The agreement on common goals would implicitly coordinate the partners' activities and fortify the impact of following public policies on the issues. All these endeavors are targeted at building a mutual understanding about ICT for development and promote a trust-based, supportive environment for establishing a technology network on alleviating intergenerational concerns. For the longer-term planning, stakeholder meetings could also help in identifying emerging issues of intergenerational concern and foster information exchange on future endeavors.

ICT enables to streamline implementation strategies and align activities internationally as well as over time. Transparency on intergenerational equity strategies helps monitor the multiple partners' contributions. Constituents will be enabled to work closely on implementing collectively-shared intergenerational goals. Local meetings need to gather participants to coordinate and govern the implementation of ICT for intergenerational equity. Regional campaigns would root ICT for development in the cultural context and thereby support an intergenerational network extension. Regional seminars and workshops should create learning experiences to foster the overall effectiveness of technology in local networks. Regional dialogues could foster the transfer of knowledge on local success patterns and generate applicable problem-solving capabilities. Information sharing on ICT best practice standards would lead to contemporary ICT solutions and prepare for future challenges.

Accountability could counterbalance a lack of clarity about the implementation of common intergenerational goals. Based on transparent activities and monitoring, benchmarking of impact assessments could identify best practice learning models for future intergenerational equity. Accountability control should also feature assessment of progress on external goals. External audits should become the basis for rewarding positive results and providing assistance in case of defaults. Non-compliance with goal accomplishment and communication deficiencies of the partners should be sanctioned – e.g., by public attention through internet channels.

All these endeavors will attract attention for intergenerational goals and gain participation from multiple stakeholders on the global level. ICT has the power to bring intergenerational considerations into the mainstream of intergovernmental debate and aid the implementation of concrete activities in a favorable intergenerational direction.

Future endeavors include the advancement of ICT at the ground level by fostering accessibility and technology use. ICT for development on the global agenda can successfully raise and support a number of constituent partnerships. ICT accessibility and harmonization of best practices standards should be fostered along the way. Local trainings and workshops could improve ICT skills and social development on the ground level. Recommendations for future developments also include linking the global level with partnership networks for a more concerted planning, strengthening of resource mobilization and setting up clearer business plans with outcome control mechanisms such as goal accomplishment checks and accountability (Puaschunder, 2017b). Regional initiatives should coordinate local action and govern the implementation of ICT for development. Transparent goal accomplishment strategies will monitor the partners' contributions. Benchmarking and impact assessments will drive best practice learning models for future PPPs.

For the future, ICT experts are advised to continue developing strong networking relationships with international organizations and local communities. Further opportunities to network and engage with a wider range of constituents in regular conferences, summits and meetings need to be explored. Innovations in ICT for development should be fostered and promoted to constituents in order to advance intergenerational leadership in the 21st century.

Chapter 6

Intergenerational Leadership

The 21st century has led to an unprecedented interdependence of massive global systems causing systemic risk to increase exponentially (Centeno et al., 2013). Emerging societal long-term downfalls have created a quest for fairness to provide an at least as favorable standard of living to future generations as enjoyed today (Puaschunder, 2015c). Global systemic risks of climate change, overindebtedness in the aftermath of the 2008/09 World Financial Crisis and the need for pension reform in the wake of an aging Western world population, currently raise attention to intergenerational fairness. Systemic transnational risks and pressing social dilemmas beyond the control of singular nation states call for corporate social activities to back governmental regulation in crisis mitigation (Puaschunder, 2015c). The following part promotes the idea of intergenerational equity in the corporate and public worlds.

6. 1. Intergenerational leadership in the corporate world

In the given literature on global responsible leadership in the corporate sector and contemporary Corporate Social Responsibility (CSR) models, intergenerational equity appears to have widely been neglected. While the notion of sustainability has been integrated into CSR models (Steurer, Martinuzzi & Margula, 2012), intergenerational equity has hardly been touched on. Intergenerational fairness differs from sustainability as for being a more legal case for codifying the triple bottom line.

Globalization led to unprecedented intergenerational equity imbalances regarding climate change, overindebtedness in the aftermath of the 2008/09 World Financial Crisis as well as pension reform needs of an aging Western world population (Puaschunder, 2015d). The outlined intergenerational equity constraints are complex and their solution interdependent. The current world economy opens possibilities but also threatens future generations.

In the eye of current intergenerational concerns, the study of global intergenerational balances leverages into a necessary and blatant demand but is up-to-date limited in order to implement intergenerational fairness.

This unprecedented intergenerational kink heralds an overall call for intergenerational equity – the fairness to provide an at least as favorable standard of living as enjoyed today. Eternal equity addresses justice over time. As an implicit contract and transfer between living and future generations, intergenerational equity not only reduces unfairness for future world inhabitants who are born in less favorable condition than their parents. Intergenerational equity also ensures future infrastructure, equal opportunities over time and constant access to social welfare for the youth.

Intergenerational equity avoids discriminating against future generations based on the remoteness of the time at which they will live. Thereby intergenerational equity grants a favorable climate for generations. Intergenerational fairness ensures climate stability and averts frictions arising from austerity plans and diminishing social welfare standards.

Intergenerational justice breeds in the social compound in the wake of intergenerational transfers within overlapping generation's networks through intergenerational connectedness and social interaction. Intergenerational mobility is enabled through intertemporal opportunities and meritocracy (Puaschunder, 2016c).

Globalization converged the concept of nation states (Held & McGrew, 2007). Nowadays the range of opportunities of what contemporary states can autonomously do is ultimately limited by their dependence on each other (Panitch & Gindin, 2012). The role of states in maintaining property rights, overseeing contracts, stabilizing currencies and reproducing class relations has gradually deteriorated in the age of internationalization. Due to global capitalism, the power and political authority have been diffused away from local state ruling to global governance. The classic ideal of the command and control state was displaced by a philosophy of economic hegemony (Held & McGrew, 2007). As multilayered economic system are structured by the strategic coordination of international corporate entities, corporate multinationals nowadays have turned to solve global societal crisis beyond the control of singular nation states.

While the trend of internationalization has weakened the power of local governance and national control, globalization has also lead to unprecedented problems of climate change, overindebtedness in the aftermath of the 2008/09 World Financial Crisis and pension reform needs of an aging Western world population. In the light of growing socio-political and environmental challenges, heightened stakeholder concern has risen attention of global stakeholders on corporate ethical conduct. In the aftermath of the 2008/09 World Financial Crisis, corporations are under scrutiny for societal contributions and corporate board managers increasingly respected for corporate social conduct with stakeholders playing a conspicuous role in influencing the interaction between governments and business. The corporate world is nowadays more than ever urged to consider the needs of a wider range of stakeholders in their decision-making, go beyond ethical requirements and outperform responsibility expectations within the surge of a positive organizational scholarship movement.

In the age of heightened shareholder and stakeholder activism towards corporate social endeavors, the time is ripe to investigate the potential of corporate activities to engage on intergenerational equity in the aftermath of the 2008/09 World Financial Crisis. With growing socio-political and environmental challenges around the world in the domains of financial, social irresponsibility, environmental resource consumption and growing costs for an aging populace, there is increasing pressure from stakeholders – among them governments, local communities, NGOs, and society at large – that corporations and their leaders contribute to societally-attentive business practices. Access-to-information laws revolutions in the Western world have steered attention to corporate ethicality. Corporate social reporting and the engagement of stakeholders have led to the adoption of a variety of global ethical standards, which may directly affect the propensity to engage in intergenerational equity implementations. Local communities, customers, employees, and NGOs, as well as shareholders, are increasingly monitoring ethical behavior in the digital age featuring greater transparency, accessibility, and reachability of corporate conduct.

Intergenerational equity in the corporate world is an alternative to national governance and a novel extension of contemporary Corporate Social Responsibility (CSR) models. Intergenerationally responsible leadership is built on the idea that corporate executives have an obligation to incorporate needs of far-ranging constituents, including future generations. In the eye of a current pressing demand for attention to intergenerational equity in the domains of climate justice and austerity, the following part theoretically highlights the corporate world's potential to alleviate current intergenerational equity imbalances and explores intergenerational justice implementation strategies of the corporate world.

While industrialization has weakened the power of local governance and national control, globalization has also lead to unprecedented problems of climate change and overindebtedness in the aftermath of the 2008/09 World Financial Crisis. Globalization also shifted national governments' intergenerational equity implementation to international governance solutions in the corporate world (Panitch & Gindin, 2012). Nowadays pressing dilemmas beyond the control of singular nation states call for attention for intergenerational fairness and corporate social activities to back governmental crisis mitigation (Centeno et al., 2013).

In the light of growing socio-political and environmental challenges, heightened stakeholder concerns have raised the attention of global stakeholders on corporate ethical conduct in the intergenerational domain. Today's intergenerational imbalances become blatant through information provided to stakeholders. Heightened transparency in the digital age makes corporate conduct and governmental actions visible to a broad range of constituents. Local communities, customers, employees, and NGOs, as well as shareholders, are increasingly monitoring ethical behavior in the digital age featuring greater transparency, accessibility, and reachability of corporate conduct.

Especially in the aftermath of the 2008/09 World Financial Crisis, corporations have become under scrutiny for societal contributions and corporate board managers increasingly respected for corporate social conduct. Stakeholders play a conspicuous role in influencing the interaction between governments and business. The corporate world is nowadays more than ever urged to consider the needs of a wider range of stakeholders in their decision-making, go beyond ethical requirements and outperform responsibility expectations within the surge of a positive organizational scholarship movement.

With growing socio-political and environmental challenges around the world in the domains of financial social irresponsibility, environmental resource consumption and growing costs for an aging populace, there is increasing pressure from stakeholders – among them governments, local communities, NGOs, and society at large – that corporations and their leaders contribute to societally attentive business practices. Access to information law revolutions in the Western world has steered attention to corporate ethicality. Corporate social reporting and the engagement of stakeholders have led to the adoption of a variety of global ethical standards, which may directly affect the propensity to engage in intergenerational equity implementations. In the age of heightened shareholder and stakeholder activism towards corporate social endeavors, the time is ripe to investigate the potential of corporate activities to engage on intergenerational equity in the aftermath of the 2008/09 World Financial Crisis.

As multi-layered economic systems are structured by the strategic coordination of international corporate entities, corporate multinationals nowadays have turned to solve global societal crisis beyond the control of singular nation states. International trade, global capitalism and economic hegemony of corporations have led to a strategic coordination of public and private actors' awareness of intergenerational imbalances (Binder, Kriebaum, Marboe, Nowak, Reinisch & Wittich, 2014).

Intergenerational equity deficiencies subsequently are tackled in bottom-up approaches to shed light on the rights of upcoming youth, voice the needs of unborn not being present in courtrooms and lobby for favorable future conditions. Given the pressing demand for attention to climate change mitigation, overindebtedness soft landing in the aftermath of the 2008/09 World Financial Crisis as well as pension reform in the eye of an aging Western world population, the need for an introduction of intergenerational equity conscientiousness in the corporate world is blatant. In a climate of corporate governance and global challenges beyond the control of singular nation states, the idea of promoting intergenerational equity in the corporate world has reached unprecedented momentum. Departing from narrow-minded, outdated views of responsibilities of corporations only adherent to making a profit for shareholders and abiding by the law (Friedman, 1970); corporate executives nowadays are more prone to act responsibly in meeting the needs of a wide range of constituents. Apart from avoiding unethical societally harmful behavior, such as bribery, fraud and employment discrimination, corporate executives currently pro-actively engage in corporate governance practice with a wider constituency outlook, including the needs of future generations.

The future conceptualization of sustainable and responsible managerial behavior may, therefore, embrace the wider constituency range and stretch the concept of corporate responsibility to voluntary sustainability for future generations. An extended stakeholder view considers a broader set of constituencies, including future generations, in corporate decision-making with impact on the social performance and long-term viability of their organizations. A broader, social contract between business and future society may be enacted by discretionary activities that are not expected of corporations and their leaders in a moral or legal sense but directly contribute to the societal welfare and the well-being of future generations. This suggests that there is a need for a broader definition of corporate responsibility that goes beyond compliance and encompasses the obligation to contribute to societal progress in a responsible and sustainable way.

Intergenerationally responsible leadership is called for that steers intentional corporate executive actions to benefit the stakeholders of the company as well as the larger society including future generations. Intergenerational corporate leadership imbues *should-do* care for future generations alongside concerns about future society. Not simply considering avoiding unethical behavior, such as bribery, fraud and employment discrimination, but also adopting a positive and pro-active ethics lens, intergenerationally responsible leadership is an Überethical drive to consider the interests of a wider range of stakeholders (Puaschunder, 2017c). Intergenerational justice concerns of the corporate world thereby directly reach out to future world inhabitants.

Integrating intergenerational equity in CSR models in academia and practice appears as an advantageous alternative given the enormous untapped potential of Transnational Corporations and Multinational Enterprises (TC&MEs) to implement equity. Nowadays, international trade is driven by transnational corporations. As corporate entities with economic influence beyond the borders of nation states holding subsidiaries in various nations of the world (Binder et al., 2014), TC&MEs are acknowledged as international legal entities and must, therefore, abide by international law standards and fulfill international court laws (e.g., ICSID and UNCITRAL). Therefore, TC&MEs should, like nation states, consider adopting concern for intergenerational equity.

There are several advantages of TC&MEs implementing intergenerational equity as a CSR means. TC&MEs hold enormous economic potential, with the largest multi-national corporations having revenues larger than many nation states. In their corporate governance, TC&MEs leadership decision-making quickly adapts to market demands without having to reach international consensus – contrary to stakeholder engagement and international consensus negation demands of classic global governance entities such as the United National, International Monetary Fund, and the World Bank. TC&MEs are not dependent on voters – such as government officials – and can thus address intergenerational concerns faster and more flexible than governmental technocrats. In addition, TC&ME leadership may be more stable than governmental officials enacted through voting cycles – that is global corporate leaders are likely to stay longer in 'office' than their governmental counterparts.

If the corporate world adopts intergenerational equity in current CSR endeavors, it could help governmental officials in very many different ways ranging from tax ethics to first-aid global governance support. For society, acknowledging intergenerational equity in the CSR practices promises to alleviate current pressing societal predicaments of overindebtedness, social welfare reform needs and environmental threats in the wake of climate change. Investigating the possibilities to integrate a temporal dimension in contemporary CSR work, innovatively guides the implementation of financial social responsibility, environmental protection education and social welfare. For academia, applying the notion of intergenerational fairness in corporate governance models fills an up-to-date undiscovered research gap that spearheads interdisciplinary behavioral law and economic models to aid in the global corporate arena.

Most recently bounded ethicality and a scientific awareness of intertemporal decision-making inconsistencies have steered attention towards sustainability. Cutting-edge research questions arise on how a temporal perspective can be integrated into contemporary sustainability notions and how the triple bottom line can imbue a longer-term perspective into the corporate world. Solving how to overcome the negative externalities of short-termism will help averting corporate sector downfalls. Being enabled to generate predictions on how to better foresee the societal implications of future consequences of current corporate decision-making (Chakrabarty & Wang, 2012; Slaper & Hall, 2011; Slawinski & Bansal, 2012) will bring the public and private sector temporal foci closer together in order to harmoniously tackle the most pressing contemporary challenges of humankind.

Increasing and expanding CSR initiatives indicate that more and more business leaders commit their companies to contribute to the "triple bottom line" to harmoniously consider social, environmental, and economic sustainability in everyday corporate decision-making (Elkington, 1997). Respect for 'people, planet, and profits' has become a corporate necessity and industrial imperative. Corporate sustainability and social responsibility have thus emerged to unprecedented momentum in academia and practitioners' discourse. In the international arena, the UN Global Compact has raised over 10,000 members, including over 7,000 businesses in 145 countries around the world. Today business leaders tend to contribute to the creation of economic and societal progress in a globally responsible and sustainable way by means as never before experienced.

The quest for an integration of intergenerational equity in contemporary CSR models of capitalism in the 21st century is targeted at strengthening socially responsible economic market approaches. Adopting intergenerational equity in the corporate world underlines the legal case for codifying intergenerational fairness on a global basis. Contributing to interdisciplinary behavioral law and economic models in intergenerational leadership may help alleviating current intertemporal predicaments and future predictable economic, social and environmental crises. Acknowledging the untapped potential of corporate entities to address global challenges beyond the reach of singular nation states, calls for the integration of intergenerational equity into contemporary CSR models with attention to differing societal, cultural values and institutional aspects related to social responsibility and ethics. Differences in business systems, legal context, the nature of regulation and the likelihood of enforcement and punishment modes, therefore, have to be scrutinized when shaping intergenerational business ethics in the global arena.

Future research should connect the individual experience to social responsibility in order to unravel ethicality nudges. Common goal compliance is hoped to be modeled by contexts that automatically nudge corporate decision makers in an intergenerational equitable direction. Public and private sector discourse on intergenerational imbalances will help fortify the codification of intergenerational fairness on a global scale. Internationally validated intergenerational equity models will elucidate intercultural, national and regional differences in social responsibility in the intergenerational domain. The prospective findings will help imbue efficiency measures on intergenerational equity implementation through real-world relevant means. CSR advocates advanced with intergenerational conscientiousness will lead to fruitful corporate contributions for sustainable humankind alongside fostering a harmonious corporate-citizen relation.

Surpassing state-of-the-art ethical corporate leadership quests on ethically compliant behavior and avoidance of unethical corporate conduct, incorporating intergenerational equity into contemporary CSR models may extend the idea of 'positive CSR' – that is outdoing legal and ethical expectations – with respect for future constituents. Going beyond mere compliance involves actions that pro-actively promote social good, beyond what is required by law. Intergenerational corporate responsibility extends CSR as a broader social contract between business and society over time. Intergenerational equity leadership of the corporate sector defines social responsibility beyond compliance and encompasses the wider obligation to contribute to societal progress in a responsible and sustainable way. Stretching the constituency attention to future generations is based on voluntary sustainability with respect for future generations' needs to ensure the long-term viability of society.

Corporate leaders thereby pro-actively outperform legal and ethical expectations regarding the rights and needs of future generations. This positive CSR drive refers to an Überethical enhancement of societal welfare beyond the narrow scope of the current generation (Puaschunder, 2017c). As a broader definition of corporate responsibility beyond avoidance of negative downfalls, the call for responsible intergenerational leadership in the corporate world encompasses the obligation to contribute to societal progress with respect for the needs of future generations. Defining novel responsibilities with a broader social contract between business and society embraces discretionary activities that contribute to the sustainable societal welfare and thereby provides a broad range of corporate, social and societal advantages.

Knowledge of contextual factors that promote intergenerational managerial decision-making with regard to corporate sustainability and social responsibility could include favorable characteristics of the organization and aspects of the broader institutional and cultural contexts in which firms are embedded that automatically trigger intergenerational concerns. Thereby the antecedents of sustainable and responsible management at multiple levels (individual, group, organization, national context, supranational bodies) but also the interlinkages among variables should be investigated. Institutional contexts within which companies and their managers operate determine executives' responsible choices. Differences in corporate governance and legal contexts but also the nature of regulation and the likelihood of enforcement shape business ethics as well as expectations of what is considered good governance and ethical conduct in a country. Managers' responsible leadership may, therefore, vary across institutional contexts in the international arena. What may be considered as intergenerational practice in one part of the world may not be ethical state-of-the-art in another. As a consequence, corporate leaders embedded in different national systems may exhibit different intergenerational ethics. Cross-national variations in socially responsible practices could be captured in order to derive implications for organizational decision makers on their corporate responsibility. Adopted CSR strategies may be scrutinized for globally standardized, locally adapted, and transnational factors to delineate globally-consistent as well as locally-oriented intergenerational equity CSR approaches with attention to intergenerational equity.

Cross-culturally operating institutions may face challenges for intergenerational equity implementation stemming from local differences in corporate practices and social, ethical norms as well as differing thresholds to sustainable behavior. For instance, challenges arise if corporations or even nation states of the industrialized world outsource intergenerational practices (e.g., environmental pollution) into territories with weaker law enforcement and public scrutiny. These findings emphasize the need for sensitivity to local conditions, transparency along the production and value chains as well as stakeholder expectations monitoring when conducting business in different contexts. Future research may also address ethical dilemmas facing managers in the global arena and their coping strategies in order to enhance leaders' potential operating in the global arena. Research should study how to balance global and local considerations in making responsible decisions. As an implication, intergenerational CSR practices should be locally oriented and emphasize sensitivity to local conditions when conducting business in different cultural contexts.

Corporate executives with foreign subsidiaries should gain training to adapt to specific needs and circumstances of local CSR intergenerational equity customs. The role of supranational factors that influence responsible leader behavior provides further insight into the propensity to engage in intergenerational equity. With supranational institutions – such as the UN – having turned to the codification of the triple bottom line in the UN Global Compact, managers are increasingly respected for their accountability and responsibility. Insights on the influence of supranational regulatory measures and institutions (e.g., NGO activism and the enactment of the UN Global Compact) on intergenerationally responsible managerial behavior may shed light on success factors in the adoption of intergenerationally socially responsible corporate practices in the global arena. International institutions should set priorities on the corporate intergenerational equity implementation agenda. Quantitative metrics based on standardized evaluation frameworks will coordinate a global monitoring and impact assessment of the role of corporations in the intergenerational equity implementation. Indices of local, national, regional and global corporate intergenerational equity endeavors will help build public-private partnership synergies but also shed light on positive and negative externalities and trade-offs. Independent governance institutional evaluation frameworks will help streamline social, economic and environmental goals through cost-benefit analysis, life cycle cost discounting and social equality programs. Public-private partnerships will aid adaptability and flexibility in collaborations between governments, the private sector, and academia. International organizations' emergent risk and crises prevention frameworks will help reform CSR endeavors to imbue an intergenerational equity focus.

The organizational-, situational-, societal, and supranational-level determinants of responsible managerial behavior can be influenced by top management teams, policy makers, educators, and external regulators. Best practice studies in this area could shed light on how companies can systematically design and utilize human resource management practices and leadership development programs to promote responsible managerial behavior. Prospective findings may thus enhance our understanding of how companies and other stakeholders can effectively prevent, manage and control the corporate risks associated with the unethical conduct of leaders. Capturing the impact of external factors on intergenerational equitable decision-making and coping with the ethical dilemmas in leadership challenges may serve as a basis for training and development activities. The implementation of intergenerational equity could further be solicited through building corporate cultures that enhance an ethical climate.

On the corporate incentive level, intergenerational equity may be implemented through performance management and reward systems to hold managers accountable for irresponsible behavior as well as create psychological incentives to think about future consequences of current corporate conduct. Best practices studies on intergenerational equity in the corporate world will serve as corporate risk management tool to help build a culture of intergenerational CSR and foster a corporate design that pays tribute to intergenerational leadership. In building a cadre of intergenerational equity corporate leaders through corporate trainings and team building development but also corporate intergenerational performance measurement and intergenerational equity reward systems, intergenerational leadership in the corporate sector will be advanced.

At the organizational level, when recruiting, selecting and promoting managers, it is essential for organizations to understand how individual-level variables such as personality traits, motives and values may predict managers' propensity to engage in ethical behavior. For example, firms can use personality tests and integrity tests, along with interviews and assessment centers, to help determine which employees might be more likely to act irresponsibly. They can also assess applicants' attitudes and values to decide whether they will match the corporate culture, with the assumption that candidates' formal qualifications and job-related skills may not be the best predictors of responsible behavior on the job. Studying personality traits but also motives and values that steer managers' propensity to engage in intergenerational equity will allow setting up assessment centers that reveal which individuals are more likely to act irresponsibly and if the managerial ethics will likely match the corporate culture on the intergenerational equity scale.

With the underlying premises of exhibited behavior being a function of both the person and the environment in which that behavior takes place, future research may also unravel ethical decision-making under situational constraints that the broader cultural and institutional environment imposes on the adoption of sustainable and socially responsible practices. Intergenerational equity can also be imbued in corporate activities by creating and enforcing company policies and codes of conduct, supporting training and development initiatives, which are aimed at increasing moral awareness regarding future generations. Once the individual has joined the organization, induction programs, individual coaching by the supervisor, training and development programs, and other socialization practices could ensure that newcomers learn values, expected behaviors, and social knowledge that are necessary to become intergenerationally conscientious managerial leaders. In terms of communication and control systems, top management teams and governmental officials may actively promote responsible behavior and discourage irresponsible behavior by communicating ethical integrity messages. Implementing performance management and reward systems to hold managers accountable for irresponsible behavior could, in addition, create a psychologically favorable situation for intergenerational ethicality (Matten & Crane, 2005).

Overall, enhancing intergenerational social conscientiousness in the corporate world is an innovative way to unprecedentedly leverage untapped potentials to implement social welfare and environmental protection through future-oriented and socially responsible economic market approaches. Thereby averting future predictable economic, social and environmental crises serves the greater goal to ensure a future sustainable and temporally harmonious humankind. Cross-national sustainability solutions and interculturally sensitive intergenerationally equitable business practices may help imbue intergenerational equity in corporate conduct in the global arena with direct implications for today's and tomorrow's society.

6. 2. Intergenerational leadership in the public sector

Globalization has placed social and environmental concerns on managerial agendas to an increased extent while more and more managers operate in a global environment. Multidisciplinary and multilevel research approaches may, therefore, investigate the comparative and cross-national dimensions of intergenerational equity and their implications for leadership decision-making and behavior in the global arena. Interdisciplinary and multilevel research approaches could feature scientific collaborations with researchers based in different countries to investigate the comparative and cross-national dimensions of intergenerationally responsible managerial behavior. The researchers should represent different disciplinary backgrounds (economics, business, psychology, etc.), research fields (e.g., strategy, organizational behavior, and international and cross-cultural management within the field of business), methodological approaches (both qualitative and quantitative), and regional expertise (in-depth knowledge of North-American, European, and Asian business systems and institutional environments). International studies of intergenerational equity should be targeted at driving a sophisticated conceptualization of 'responsible behavior' in the intergenerational domain that is applicable to all cultural groups and stakeholders.

A wider conceptualization of intergenerational equity leadership based on comparative cross-cultural research will help detect intergenerational equity antecedents. Interdisciplinary, multilevel research will unravel drivers of intergenerational responsibility and situational influence factors on intergenerational conscientiousness in the international arena. Avenues of future research could also enhance our understanding of how companies and other stakeholders can effectively promote socially responsible behavior for future generations.

Academic research can aid to spearhead temporal perspectives in contemporary CSR research. In particular, a macroeconomic model of global intergenerational equity could study intertemporal transfers between generations with special attention to public and private sector contributions as well as benefit and burden sharing. Based on the intergenerational equity dimensions of social responsibility and future orientation, public and private sector intergenerational benefit transfers and burden sharing will thereby capture social, environmental and economic intergenerational contribution potentials of the corporate world and global governance. Cross-cultural differences could be outlined by cross-sectional regression analyses on a global scale.

The age of globalization heralded the call for responsible intergenerational leadership. With internationalization trends imposing significant challenges regarding the sustainability of climate stability, indebtedness and social welfare for an aging Western world population, the need for intergenerationally responsible leadership in the public sector has leveraged into an international concern.

In the sustainability domain, research, therefore, may set out to investigate how to bear the burden of climate taxation in a fair and just way in the climate change burden-sharing context. Finding the optimum balance between consumption tax adjusted for income levels through a progressive tax scheme will unravel drivers of tax compliance in the sustainability domain. If climate taxation is perceived as the fair and just allocation of the climate burden, this should help convince taxpayers to pay one's share to avert global warming. A novel 'service-and-client' atmosphere could promote taxpayers as cooperative citizens that would be willing to comply voluntarily if they perceive their share as a fair contribution to a collectively enjoyed stable environment. This strategy of taxpayer collaboration promotion could ultimately enhance tax morale in the environmental domain. Contemporary climate taxation schemes should be studied descriptively coupled with economic cost-benefit analyses. Information is advised to be collected on taxation aiding climate change risk mitigation and adaptation strategies with a special emphasis on the finance sector.

In order to finance climate change mitigation and adaptation efforts, a diversified taxation scheme is proposed. Climate justice *within* a country acknowledges adjusting climate taxation for consumption and income levels as well as past environmental damaging behavior to find a fair distribution of the burden of climate change. The idea is to share the burden of climate taxation in a mix of (1) consumption tax, (2) progressive tax and (3) inheritance tax.

A carbon tax on top of the existing tax system could reduce the burden of climate change and ultimately allow clean economic growth through subsidies for clean energy. Carbon emission consumption tax appears just in light of placing a heavier burden on those who engage in activities that offset climate change. A consumption tax can also curb harmful emissions and directly nudge behavior towards sustainability. Yet, to place a fair share of the burden of climate change mitigation upon society, these taxes have to be adjusted to the income level of individuals in order to not charge low-income heavier than deep pocket households.

Besides progressive taxation schemes to imbue a sense of fairness in climate change burden sharing, inheritance taxation is a creative means to reap past wealth accumulation, which potentially offset and caused past environmental damage. Allocating the burden of climate change mitigation and adaptation in a fair way within society will therefore also feature research on contemporary inheritance tax structures in place and their role in financing the climate stability agenda. Retroactive taxation of past wealth accumulation at the expense of environmental damage through inheritance tax will be legally justified.

Empirically, future research should comprise of a macroeconomic tax revenue cost-benefit analysis to find the optimum solution on how to distribute the taxation burden within society. The analysis should cover consumption tax, progressive tax, and inheritance taxation and aim at estimating the optimum taxation mix to ensure the burden of climate abatement and adaptation costs are distributed in a fair manner within society.

When comparing the burden of climate change distributed throughout the world, legal arguments from the past may be subsumed to ensure a fair and just solution for tomorrow's climate stability. In the past, private property rights were in some cases weakened for establishing common goods for the greater good. If the possessor of goods was not alive anymore and previously private goods would be turned into public goods for the greater good, private property rights could be overruled. Using argumentation points of the unknown possessor of tomorrow's stable climate but also drawing attention to the benefits of the common good of a favorable climate will be the main argumentation to decide how to distribute the burden of climate stability among different countries in a fair manner throughout the world. Countries with higher access to a stable climate and more population will be argued to necessarily having to bear a higher share of climate change abatement. Those countries that have a competitive advantage of a warming earth will be argued to having to redistribute their gains to parts of the world, where climate change causes harm, e.g., such as in the case of climate refugees. Based on legal assumptions, argumentations of the first world having better means of protection and conservation of a stable climate, will lead to insights on natural differences between the developed and the undeveloped parts of the world and therefore naturally differing responsibilities to protect a stable climate.

The legal argumentation about climate stability touches on different fields of law, ranging from common goods to private property to human rights. While climate was historically understood as a common good, which is non-excludable and non-rivalrously shared and beneficial for all world members, this perception is currently challenged by climate change. If climate becomes less stable, climate may not be considered as common good anymore. For instance, if climate instability impacts certain world areas by weather extremes such as sea level rise, flooding, droughts, desert formation, storms, and hurricanes more severe than other parts of the world that may even benefit from a warmer climate (e.g., consider Russia's and Canada's access to natural resources when ice is melting in their Northern territories), a quest for living in a beneficial area of the world may leverage a favorable climate as a quasi-luxury. Living in a part of the world with a beneficial climate may become an exclusive privilege that is rivalrously contested. Under these circumstances, the climate would not be considered as classical common good. But also take the example of rising sea levels. If the climate gets warmer, sea levels rise and drown landscape under water; the common good of climate directly affects private property. Predictions of Venice disappearing and Manhattan being almost by half under water in 200 years[1] if we continue on business as usual path, underline the direct impact of the common good climate on private property rights. If the temperature rises, private property will be destroyed or more expensive to maintain than before.

Climate justice concerns also directly touch on human rights. Climate justice links human rights and sustainable development to safeguard the rights of those affected by climate change. The claim for a human right of access to a stable climate stems from intergenerational fairness demands, which is a natural behavioral law or a human imbued cue that has been practiced ever since (Puaschunder, 2015c). The greater goal of ensuring climate justice is that not one generation creates irreversible lock-ins for future generations. Considerations of a stable climate being connected to human rights have leveraged into a blatant demand in the light of changing sea levels. Climate refugees are not treated under the Geneva Convention[2] as long as their rights are not traced back to a human right. From the Arctic to the Indian Ocean to the South Pacific, small island states and coastal lines have therefore nowadays become home to the most vulnerable communities, whose rights are not fully protected by contemporary legal frameworks, as their decision is not fully legally considered. The threat of rising sea levels in the wake of climate change pushes populations to relocate to safer areas. Contemporary legal frameworks do not recognize and protect the rights of climate migrants. Climate refugees do not fall under Geneva Convention[3] protectorate. Climate justice may thus be leveraged as a human right in the years to follow in subsequent legislation to ensure a decent standard of living of those affected by climate change.

As the destabilization of climate will directly destroy, damage or intensify maintenance costs of private property and decent living; the climate stabilization efforts therefore also have entered private property and standard of living financialization considerations. In the financing of climate stabilization, the

---

[1] http://www.businessinsider.com/map-shows-how-much-of-nyc-could-be-underwater-in-200-years-2015-7

[2] https://www.icrc.org/en/war-and-law/treaties-customary-law/geneva-conventions

[3] https://www.icrc.org/en/war-and-law/treaties-customary-law/geneva-conventions

private market rationale has been proposed following World Bank and United Nations approaches to price natural resources. These financialization and commodification of nature efforts, however, have just started. In the commodification of climate, the economic rationale should be applied but with the caution of legal oversight. The basic economic rules of supply and demand suggest that an over-demand of climate elevates the price of a stable climate. Legal rationale following the quest for justice between countries subsumes the rising price of a stable climate to those countries that benefit more from a stable climate, should also be paying a higher price for climate stabilization. Fair climate change burden-sharing between countries could, therefore, comprise of two argumentations: First, those countries who benefit more from a stable climate – hence those with a larger landscape or higher population, who have more access to climate than others and hence a greater summed up utility over all their individual nationals derived from a stable climate should also bear a higher degree of the burden of climate change mitigation and adaptation efforts. Second, those countries who benefit more from global warming and reap benefits from a warmer earth temperature should redistribute some of the wealth accumulation due to climate change to offset the costs arising from global warming at other countries of the world that suffer from a decline in living conditions due to rising temperatures. The legal foundation for different country approaches toward climate mitigation, and adaptation cost sharing can be found at the heart of sustainability having been declared as one in which countries have 'common but differentiated responsibilities,'[4] which was first discussed in Principle 7 of the Rio Declaration at the first Rio Earth Summit in 1992.[5] New to this argument, however, is that the benefits of global warming – which are real and exist, for instance, in melting ice allowing unprecedented access to below surface resources and larger arable landscape – should be shared globally to offset costs and harms produced from a higher temperature in other parts of the world (Puaschunder, 2017a).

In addition, building on the case and international law, those countries that have better means of protection or conservation of the common climate should also face a greater responsibility to protect the earth. The legal basis for this argument stems from an inverted subsumption of the argumentation whether climate stability is a common good or impacts on private property and draws on historical cases of legally justified expropriation. Private

---

4 http://cisdl.org/public/docs/news/brief_common.pdf

5 http://www.unep.org/documents.multilingual/default.asp?documentid=78&articleid=1163

property rights are some of the starkest legal claims existent around the world. Private property rights hold through time, distance and space. If a neighbor goes on vacation, one cannot simply move in his home and claim oneself as sole possessor. But there is one interesting case in history, where private property rights could be neglected for the sake of common goods. In history, the private property claim of a country was legally justified negligible if (1) those who possessed a good were not alive anymore and direct attribution of the possessor non-existent; (2) the former private property was turned into a common good; and (3) the new possessors had better means of protection and conservation than the good had experienced before. Take historical examples such as the Stone of Rosetta but also other cases such as the 'Elgin' Parthenon Marbles as part of the Athenian Acropolis (Downs, 2008). Historically the Stone of Rosetta was discovered by Napoleon Bonaparte in 1799 in the small town of Rosetta in Egypt and is now exhibited in the British Museum for more than 200 years. There are several arguments for not restituting former private property to the countries of their origin as in the case of the Stone of Rosetta: (1) The *actual former possessors* are not alive anymore and unknown, which transposes any direct individual property claim to the international law domain, hence the country Egypt contests the country Great Britain over possession. Great Britain claims (2) to turn the former private property to a common good through granting a *large and diverse group access*. London – as a vibrant metropolitan hub with a vast array of visitors – is a better stage to explain the meaning of the stone to a broader public than if the stone were still in Rosetta, a small town near Alexandria in Egypt. The display of the stone in a museum adds additional value: (3) The British Museum has better *means of protection, preservation and conservation* of the stone than if it were displayed by itself in a desert town benefiting not only from the political stability of Great Britain but also the strong culture of heritage tradition conservation as a Royal mandate. (4) The surrounding in a museum grants the stone meaning and a *Gestalt* bringing to life the mysteries of the ancient Egypt and the stone's importance as a historical artefact in deciphering Greek, Hieroglyphs and demotic Egyptian (Downs, 2008). The stone's connection to history truly becomes apparent in the wealth of other displayed objects that bestow upon the stone a certain collective value. The sum of objects in a museum is worth more in its entirety than its sole pieces standing alone.

Instead of asking whether ancient colonial claims have still today the right to retain misplaced cultural heritage, the argumentations on which the justification for these items to remain in former colonial powers could be subsumed to the novel and contemporary case of climate protection. In the arguments if the first and the second world should bear the same burden of climate change mitigation and adaptation efforts brought up foremost by

China arguing to have a right to economic growth by the same – unfortunately climate-change causing – means of economic transition as the first world had in previous centuries,[6] one could subsume from the above case of expropriation for the sake of common goods creation: (1) That climate change will potentially infringe on private property rights of *future possessors* who are currently unknown. (2) Those countries should bear a higher burden of climate change mitigation and adaptation efforts that have *more access to climate*, hence those with a larger landscape and/or those with a larger population; (3) but also those countries who have better means of *protection, preservation, and conservation*, hence the first world may have to take on a greater responsibility in averting climate change. (4) There is a natural *Gestalt* over time regarding climate. Over time, the sum of a stable climate over time is more precious than the individual generation's costs incurred to maintain a favorable climate. Shedding light at these deficiencies underlines the need for considering climate justice a natural law over time that connects the past to our common future (Puaschunder, 2015c).

6. 3. International organizations' lead on intergenerational coordination

As the main factors contributing to intergenerational imbalances are complex and can either stem from the local, regional, national or international but also the intertemporal level, global governance coordination of intergenerational leadership on the global governance level is recommended. While climate change is a global issue, overindebtedness is a country-specific factor. Although the origins of these two different problems vary, as well as their implications over intergenerational transfers are of very different nature, intergenerational organizations seem the optimal entities to adopt a global governance viewpoint that unveils their overlapping contents and interdependencies. International research on intergenerational equity in the international organization domain could determine drivers of intergenerationally responsible managerial behavior. Cross-national, multi-level analyses could thereby retrieve influence factors on the adoption of globally responsible intergenerational leadership and corporate practices.

Since 2008 the International Law Commission of the United Nations has been promoting intergenerational equity primarily on global governance issues – such as climate change awareness, overindebtedness, and pension

6 http://dotearth.blogs.nytimes.com/2009/12/23/views-on-china-and-copenhagen/?_r=0

reform – to the public sector. The implementation of intergenerational equity in this domain, though, seems to be slowed by an ongoing discussion of whether international law can overrule nation states' sovereignty. The debate has just recently started and may not come to a satisfactory end in the near future.

In the international arena, the UN Global Compact has raised over 10,000 members, including over 7,000 businesses in 145 countries around the world (Puaschunder, 2010). Increasing and expanding Corporate Social Responsibility (CSR) initiatives indicate that more and more business leaders commit their companies to contribute to the "triple bottom line" to harmoniously considers social, environmental, and economic sustainability in everyday corporate decision-making (Elkington, 1997). Respect for 'people, planet, and profits' has become a corporate necessity and industrial imperative. Corporate sustainability and social responsibility have thus emerged to unprecedented momentum in academia and practitioners' discourse. Today business leaders tend to contribute to the creation of economic and societal progress in a globally responsible and sustainable way by means as never before experienced.

Most recently the World Bank and Peace Institute have shown grown interest in behavioral insights. For instance, the World Bank has established a nudging unit, which became essential in writing the 2015 World Development Report (2015). The US-based Peace Institute hosted a White House behavioral economics retreat in December 2016. Around the globe, behavioral insights are used by many governments to nudge citizens into socially favorable outcomes. In addition, public central national banks are currently starting to develop an interest in climate bonds.

Chapter 7

Discussion, Conclusion, Future Outlook

Intergenerational responsibility is as old as humankind. Climate change, over-indebtedness of nation states and an aging Western world population, however, has leveraged the demand for intergenerational equity to unprecedented momentum. Overall, in the eye of an unprecedented intergenerational equity kink, it has become economically efficient to think about the next generation and future world-inhabitants' living conditions.

Future research avenues may pay attention to the driving forces of normative ideals of intergenerational equity to understand the meaning and motivations behind the topic of interest, among different stakeholders. For example, more detailed information is certainly needed in order to capture differences in the emphasis given to the social representations of intergenerational equity between economics and finance elites, and public servants and international organizations.

Future studies might investigate the change of social representations on intergenerational equity as well as take into account country-level differences in intertemporal policy-making during other times of economic cycles. Additional follow-up investigations may also unravel the current dynamics of the local civil society in establishing intergenerational justice, despite the international forces leading towards globalization, financialization or pension privatization (Puaschunder & Schwarz, 2012; Puaschunder, 2015a, b).

Attention could be paid to the importance of prevailing county-level mechanisms for the interplay of different institutions, economic and financial market actors, as well as welfare state representatives that respectively affect the representations and implementation of intergenerational equity (Puaschunder, 2015c, d). Cross-national variations in pension reforms are prime examples of different thresholds of intergenerational equity. But also potential crowding out effects between public and private sector intergenerational justice implementation strategies are planned to be explored in the future (Puaschunder, 2015a).

Additional research may also capture intergenerational conscientiousness in other parts of the world. For instance, an intercultural variation could investigate a Chinese sample representing a youth with unprecedented prosperity. Reflecting the flipside of the Western world trade deficit, the Asian supply side population currently faces an unprecedented increase in access to capital and opportunities. Intercultural comparisons of intergenerational equity perceptions could thereby help explaining which features of intergenerational equity are universal to humankind in order to retrieve human-imbued intergenerational equity success factors (Puaschunder & Schwarz, 2012).

Intercultural comparisons could also prove the international stability and global validity of intergenerational equity nudges as a global public policy tool (Puaschunder & Schwarz, 2012; 2015b). Testing the intercultural applicability of social representations on intergenerational concerns around the globe will thus help implementing intergenerational equity and instigate intertemporal transfers on a grand scale (Puaschunder, 2016d).

Overall, the presented research offers several contributions in the emerging field of law, economics, and governance. Describing social representations spearheads sociology entering economics. Intergenerational equity introduced as a natural behavioral law serves as a basis for future-oriented and socially responsible codification and regulation. Research connecting the individual experience to social responsibility allows to innovatively unravel ethicality nudges (Thaler & Sunstein, 2008).

Common goal compliance on intergenerational responsibility is hoped to be modeled by the information retrieved on the social representations of intergenerational equity. Gaining acceptance for future societal contributions will help legislators to automatically nudge decision makers into an intergenerational equitable direction and thereby foster a harmonious government-citizen relation following the greater goal of ensuring a sustainable humankind.

Governments must breed hope through forward-looking strategies in the eye of radical austerity cuts and unemployment gaps to take away people's fear of the future. Policy makers are pressured to revise social services. While intergenerational equity concerns are as old as humankind – the 2008/09 World Financial Crisis has put a new stance on the dimensions of overindebtedness and irreversible destruction of future potential, which may serve as an explanation for 2011 occupy Zeitgeist reclaiming public space as a symbol for common goods. In the eye of leaving next generations' debt, unfeasible social welfare and sustainability threats, intergenerational equity is an urgent topic of concern.

While the wish for intergenerational equity has sparked, we currently lack a codified legal framework on intergenerational fairness as well as an economic understanding of feasible intergenerational equity models that accurately pay attention to future generations. To measure intergenerational equity, we will have to estimate future developments. Intergenerational equity will require discounting of future events by politicians, policy makers and private individuals who will have to factor in future-orientation and social responsibility in current decisions. Future world inhabitants must be put into the focus of today's choices by shifting the current wealth of the elderly to save for future generations and put sustainable governance in place. We may also have to curb our consumption rates to transmit the earth's resources to future generations conscientiously.

The balance between the welfare of present and future generations can also be established through spontaneous and individual saving decision of the present generation as well as policy implementations of this preference-seeking to arrange tax collection and governmental actions affecting the economy to distort or amend the individual saving preferences in favor of future generations (Bauer, 1957). Social discount rates weight the well-being of future generations relative to those alive today. Society can use intergenerational fiscal transfers to allocate the burdens across generations without the need to trade off from generation's well-being for another's (Sachs, 2014).

While classic economic models portrayed balancing the interests of different generations as ethical or political problem of competitive markets and state governance alike (Allais, 1947) and some economists even opposed discounting of future utilities (Harrod, 1948; Ramsey, 1928); nowadays, intergenerational equity has become a political question of how far democracy goes and temporal justice an ethical obligation for the future. But when considering the current inequality over time, we face legal adaptations not instantly applying to current external changes. Beyond lagging legal codifications and yet to be adjusted policy frameworks, we must strive for understanding natural expressions of intergenerational equity and core humane values of justice as a responsibility for the future. Sustainability intuitions should be explored.

Eternal equity has always been lived within the family compound and practiced in the wake of humane fairness notions. The human-imbued wish to provide an at least as the favorable standard of living to our children stems from evolutionary, social and religious values. Ignorance regarding intergenerational concerns naturally feels wrong, and hegemony of now appears like a sin on future generations. Not being intergenerationally conscientious puts offspring at stake and detaches people from their environment. Further understanding intergenerational conscientiousness as a natural behavioral humane-imbued law will help integrating future conditions in today's decision-making.

Overall, we must cultivate the human-imbued Überethical drive towards intergenerational conscientiousness that was argued as the basis of eternal equity. Building on Rawls' (1971) procedural justice, intergenerational equity will ensure fairness between generations based on future orientation and social responsibility. Pursuing intergenerational equity in the wish to provide a decent standard of living for the upcoming young can be enabled by a mutual transfer between old and young. Constituting intergenerational harmony in legal foundations, public policies, and regulation but also echoing in bottom-up participatory democracy and social representations of intergenerational equity will aid a right, just and fair distribution of assets, equity, and burdens over time. Justice should also be sought in future outlooks, humane reflexivity and globalized solidarity enabling that one generation does not live at the expense of future generations. Financial Social Responsibility will aid that the current generation is not spending the money of tomorrow's children or destabilizes a favorable world climate. Generations passing on to the future will feature age-attentively redistributed wealth, investments for young and respect for future generations' environmental resources needs. All these endeavors are targeted at cultivating a cherishing zest for the balanced well-being of this generation and the ones to come in order to ensure a harmonious, constantly evolving and sustainable humankind.

References

Adams, J. S. (1965). Inequity in social exchange. In K. Berkowitz (Ed.), *Advances in Experimental Social Psychology,* pp. 267-299, New York, N.Y.: Academic Press.

Adler, N. E., Epel, E. S., Castellazzo, G. & Ickovics, J. R. (2000). Relationship of subjective and objective social status with psychological and physiological functioning: Preliminary data in healthy, White women. *Health Psychology, 19,* 6, 586-592.

Aja, A., Bustillo, D., Darity, W. & Hamilton, D. (2013). Jobs instead of austerity: A bold policy proposal for economic justice. *Social Research: An International Quarterly, 80,* 3, 781-794.

Allais, M. (1947). *Economie et intérét.* Imprimerie Nationale, Paris, France.

Arrow, K., Bowles, S. & Durlauf, St. (1999). *Meritocracy and economic inequality.* Princeton, N. J.: Princeton University Press.

Ashenfelter, O. & Krueger, A. (1994). Estimates of the economic return to schooling from a new sample of twins. *American Economic Review, 84,* 5, 1157-1172.

Atkinson, A. B., Maynard, A. K. & Trinder, C. G. (1983). *Parents and children: Incomes in two generations.* London, U.K.: Heinemann.

Axelrod, R. (1984). *The evolution of cooperation.* New York, N.Y.: Basic Books.

Bales, R. F. (1951). Channels of communication in small groups. *American Sociological Review, 16,* 461-468.

Ball, S. B. & Eckel, C. C. (1996). Buying status: Experimental evidence on status in negotiation. *Psychology & Marketing, 13,* 4, 381-405.

Barnosky, A. D., Matzke, N., Tomiya, S., Wogan, G. O. U., Swartz, B., Quental, T. B., Marshall, Ch., McGuire, J. L., Lindsey, E. L., Maguire, K. C., Mersey, B. & Ferrer, E. A. (2011). Has the earth's sixth mass extinction already arrived? *Nature, 471,* 51-57.

Baron, J. (1998). *Judgment misguided: Intuition and error in public decision-making.* New York, N.Y.: Oxford University Press.

Baron, J., Bazerman, M. H. & Shonk, K. (2006). Enlarging the societal pie through wise legislation: A psychological perspective. *Perspectives on Psychological Science, 1,* 123-132.

Bauer, P. T. (1957). *Economic analysis and policy in underdeveloped countries.* Chapel Hill: Duke University Press.

Bazerman, M. H. & Chugh, D. (2005). Bounded awareness: Focusing failures in negotiation. In L. Thompson (Ed.), *Frontiers of Social Psychology: Negotiation,* pp. 7-26, New York, N.Y.: Psychological Press.

Bazerman, M. H., Loewenstein, G. & White, S. B. (1992). Reversals of preference in interpersonal decision-making: The difference between judging an alternative and choosing between multiple alternatives. *Administrative Science Quarterly, 37,* 220-240.

Bazerman, M. H. & Moore, D. A. (2008). *Judgment in managerial decision-making.* New York, N.Y.: Wiley.

Bazerman, M. H., Moore, D. A., Tenbrunsel, A. E., Wade-Benzoni, K. A. & Blount, S. (1999). Explaining how preferences change across joint versus separate evaluation. *Journal of Economic Behavior & Organization, 39,* 41-58.

Bazerman, M. H., Schroth, H., Pradhan, P., Diekmann, K. & Tenbrunsel, A. (1994). The inconsistent role of comparison others and procedural justice in reactions to hypothetical job descriptions: Implications for job acceptance decisions. *Organizational Behavior and Human Processes, 60,* 326-352.

Bazerman, M. H. & Tenbrunsel, A. E. (2011). *Blind spots: Why we fail to do what is right and what to do about it.* Princeton, N.J.: Princeton University Press.

Becker, G. (1976). Altruism, egoism, and genetic fitness: Economics and sociobiology. *Journal of Economic Literature, 14,* 817-826.

Becker, G. S. (1988). Family economics and the inheritance of inequality. *American Economic Review, 78,* 1, 1-13.

Becker, G. & Tomes, N. (1986). Human capital and the rise and fall of families. *Journal of Labor Economics, 4,* 4, 1-39.

Benke, N. & Meissel, F. -St. (2008). *Übungsbuch Römisches Sachenrecht.* Vienna: Manz.

Berger, J. M. & Zelditch, M. J. (1985). *Status, rewards, and influence.* San Francisco: Jossey Bass.

Binder, Ch., Kriebaum, U., Marboe, I., Nowak, M., Reinisch, A. & Wittich, St. (2014). *Völkerrecht.* Vienna: University of Vienna Faculty of Law Juridicum.

Bird, C. (2004). Status, identity, and respect. *Political Theory, 32,* 2, 207-232.

Borjas, G. (1995). Ethnicity, neighborhoods, and human capital externalities. *American Economic Review, 85,* 3, 365-390.

Boscov-Ellen, D. (2015). Lecture notes. GECO 5250: *Rethinking capitalism.* Spring 2015. New York, N.Y.: The New School.

Bouchard, T. J. & McGue, M. (1981). Familial studies of intelligence: A review. *Science, 212,* 4498, 1055-1059.

Bourdieu, P. (1979/1984). *Distinction: A social critique of the judgement of taste.* London, U.K.: Routledge.

Bowles, S., Gintis, H. & Osborne, M. (2008). *Unequal chances: Family background and economic success.* Princeton, N.J.: Princeton University Press.

Boyer, R. (2012). The four fallacies of contemporary austerity policies: The lost Keynesian legacy. *The Cambridge Journal of Economics, 36,* 1, 283-312.

Brasington, D., Kato, M. & Semmler, W. (2010). Transitioning out of poverty. *Metroeconomica: International Review of Economics, 61,* 1, 68-95.

Broome, J. (1999). *Ethics out of economics.* Cambridge, M.A.: Cambridge University Press.

Cass, D. & Yaari, M. (1967). Individual saving, aggregate capital accumulation and efficient growth. In K. Shell (Ed.), *Essays on the Theory of Optimal Growth*, pp. 233-268, Cambridge, M.A.: MIT Press.

Centeno, M. A., Cinlar, E., Cloud, D., Creager, A. N., DiMaggio, P. J., Dixit, A. K., Elga, A. N., Felten, E. W., James, H., Katz, St. N., Keohane, R. O., Leonard, Th. C., Massey, W. A., Mian, A. R., Mian, Z., Oppenheimer, M., Shafir, E. & Shapiro, J. N. (2013). *Global systemic risk.* Unpublished manuscript for research community. Princeton Institute for International and Regional Studies, Princeton University, April 2013.

Centeno, M. A. & Tham, A. (2012). *The emergence of risk in the global system.* Working paper, Princeton University.

Chakrabarty, S. & Wang, L. (2012). The long-term sustenance of sustainability practices in MNCs: A dynamic capabilities perspective of the role of R&D and internationalization. *Journal of Business Ethics, 110*, 2, 205-217.

Chance, E. (1967). Group psychotherapy in community mental health programs. *American Journal of Orthopsychiatry, 37*, 5, 920-925.

Charles, K. K. & Hurst, E. (2002). *The correlation of wealth across generations.* Working paper, University of Chicago.

Chernev, A. (2009). *Goal orientation and consumer preference for the status quo.* Retrievable at http://www.ssrn.com/.

Chetty, R., Hendren, N. & Katz, L. F. (2015). *The effects of exposure to better neighborhoods on children: New evidence from the moving to opportunity experiment.* Working paper, National Bureau of Economic Research.

Cole, H., Mailath, G. & Postlewaite, A. (1992). Social norms, savings behavior, and growth. *Journal of Political Economy, 100*, 6, 1092-1125.

Coleman, J. S. (1990). *Foundations of social theory.* Cambridge, M.A.: Harvard University Press.

Cooper, S., Durlauf, St. & Johnson, P. (1994). On the evolution of economic status across generations. *American Economic Review, 84*, 2, 50-58.

Corak, M. & Heisz, A. (1999). The intergenerational earnings and income mobility of Canadian men: Evidence from the longitudinal income tax data. *Journal of Human Resources, 34*, 3, 505-533.

Currim, I. S. & Sarin, R. K. (1989). Prospect versus utility. *Management Science, 35*, 1, 22-41.

deRosa, A. S. (1994). From theory to metatheory in social representations: The lines of argumentation of a theoretical-methodological debate. *Social Science Information, 33*, 273-304.

de Sam, M., Dougan, B., Gordon, J., Puaschunder, J. & St. Clair, C. (2008). *Building a globally competent citizenry in the United States.* Washington, D.C.: United States Department of Education.

Diamond, P. (1965). National debt in a neoclassical growth model. *American Economic Review, 55*, 5, 1126-1150.

DiTella, R., Haisken-DeNew, J. & MacCulloch, R. (2001). *Happiness adaptation to income and to status in an individual panel.* Working paper, Harvard Business School.

Downs, J. (2008). *Discovery of Rosetta: The stone that unlocked the mysteries of ancient Egypt.* London, U.K.: Constable & Robinson.

Duesenberry, J. S. (1949). *Income, saving and the theory of consumer behavior.* Cambridge, M.A.: Harvard University Press.

Durkheim, E. (1898). *Représentations individuelles et répresentations collectives. Sociologie et philosophie.* Paris, France: Presses Universitaires de France.

Durlauf, St. (2001). A framework for the study of individual behavior and social interaction. *Sociological Methodology, 31,* 1, 47-87.

Dymski, G. (2013). The logic and impossibility of austerity. *Social Research: An International Quarterly, 80,* 3, 665-696.

Easterlin, R. A. (1974). *Does economic growth improve the human lot? Some empirical evidence.* New York, N.Y.: Academic Press.

Elkington, J. (1997). *Cannibals with forks: The triple bottom line of twenty-first-century business.* Oxford, UK.: Capstone.

el Sehity, T., Hoelzl, E. & Kirchler, E. (2005). Price developments after a nomial shock: Benford's law and psychological pricing after the Euro introduction. *International Journal of Research in Marketing, 22,* 4, 471-480.

Erikson, R. & Goldthorpe, J. H. (1992). *The constant flux: A study of class mobility in the industrial societies.* Oxford, UK.: Oxford University Press.

Eurostat retrieved at http://ec.europa.eu/eurostat/web/lucas/data/primary-data/2015

Falkenstein, E. (2006). *Why risk and return are uncorrelated: A relative status approach.* Working paper, Eden Prairie, Telluride Asset Management.

Fan, E. T. & Gruenfeld, D. H. (1998). When needs outweigh desires: The effects of resource interdependence and reward interdependence on group problem solving. *Basic and Applied Social Psychology, 20,* 45-56.

Feld, L. P. & Frey, B. S. (2005). Illegal, immoral, fattening or what? How deterrence and responsive regulation shape tax morale. In C. Bajada & F. Schneider (Eds.), *Size, Causes and Consequences of the Underground Economy,* pp. 16-37, Aldershot: Ashgate.

Festinger, L. (1954). A theory of social comparison processes. *Human Relations, 7,* 117-140.

Foley, D. K. (2009). The economic fundamentals of global warming. In J. M. Harris & N. R. Goodwin (Eds.), *Twenty-first Century Macroeconomics: Responding to the Climate Challenge,* pp. 115-126, Cheltenham: Edward Elgar.

Fox, S. & Dayan, K. (2004). Framing and risky choice as influenced by comparison of one's achievements with others: The case of investment in the stock exchange. *Journal of Business and Psychology, 18,* 3, 301-321.

Fraser, N. (2014). Can society be commodities all the way down? Post-Polanyian reflections on capitalist crisis. *Economy and Society, 43,* 4, 441-458.

Frey, B. S. (2003). Deterrence and tax morale in the European Union. *European Review, 11,* 3, 385-406.

Friedman, M. (1953). Choice, chance and the personal distribution of income. *Journal of Political Economy, 61,* 4, 277-290.

Friedman, M. (1970). The social responsibility of business is to increase its profits. New York: *The New York Times,* September 13.

Friedman, M. & Savage, L. J. (1948). The utility analysis of choices involving risk. *Journal of Political Economy, 56*, 4, 279-304.

Galiani, S. & Weinschelbaum, F. (2007). *Social status and corruption.* Retrievable at
http://www.idec.gr/iier/new/corruption%20conference/Social%20Status%20and%20Corruption%20-%20Federico%20Weinschelbaum.pdf

García, P. F., Martínez, L. S. & Radoselovics, J. F. G. (2008). *Estimation of social capital in the world: Time series by country.* Fundación BBVA: Documentos de Trabajo.

Ghilarducci, T. (2005). Female dual labor markets and employee benefits. *Scottish Journal of Political Economy, 52*, 1, 18-37.

Ghilarducci, T. (2013). Austerity distorts the common economic interest between generations. *Social Research: An International Quarterly, 80*, 3, 953-976.

Ghilarducci, T. & McGahey, R. (2013). Editor's introduction *Social Research: An International Quarterly, 80*, 3, 21-22.

Goldberger, A. (1989). Economic and mechanical models of intergenerational transmission. *American Economic Review, 79*, 3, 504-513.

Gourville, J. T. & Soman, D. (2005). Overchoice and assortment type: When and why variety backfires. *Marketing Science, 24*, 3, 295-382.

Greenacre, M. (2007). Constructing maps of data using correspondence analysis. *BBVA Foundation Newsletter, 6*, 16-17.

Gujarati, D. N. & Porter, D. C. (2009). *Basic econometrics.* New York, N.Y.: McGraw-Hill.

Guryan, J., Hurst, E. & Kearney, M. (2008). *Parental education and parental time with children.* Cambridge, M.A.: National Bureau of Economic Research.

Güth, W. & Tietz, R. (1990). Ultimatum bargaining behavior: A survey and comparison of experimental results. *Journal of Economic Psychology, 11*, 417-449.

Harbaugh, R. (2006). *Prospect theory or skill signaling?* Retrievable at http://papers.ssrn.com/sol3/papers.cfm?abstract_id=311409.

Harrod, R. F. (1948). *Towards a dynamic economics.* London, U.K.: Macmillan.

Held, D. & McGrew, A. G. (2007). *A new world economic order? Global markets and state power: Beyond globalization/anti-globalization: Beyond the great divide.* New York, N.Y.: Polity.

Hill, R. C., Griffiths, W. E. & Lim, G. C. (2012). *Principles of econometrics.* London, U.K.: Wiley.

Hong, K. & Bohnet, I. (2004). *Status and distrust: The relevance of inequality and betrayal aversion.* RWP04-041. Working paper, Harvard Kennedy School.

Hopkins, E. & Kornienko, T. (2004). Running to keep the same place: Consumer choice as a game of status. *American Economic Review, 94*, 4, 1085-1107.

Horberg, E. J., Oveis, C. & Keltner, D. (2011). Emotions as moral amplifiers: An appraisal tendency approach to the influences of distinct emotions upon moral judgments. *Emotion Review, 3*, 237-244.

House, R. J., Hanges, P. J., Javidan, M., Dorfman, P. W. & Gupta, V. (2004). *Culture, leadership, and organizations: The GLOBE study of 62 societies.* Thousand Oaks: Sage Publications.

Howell, D. R. (2013). The austerity of low pay: US exceptionalism in the age of inequality. *Social Research: An International Quarterly, 80,* 3, 795-816.

Huberman, B. A., Loch, Ch. & Önçüler, A. (2004). Status as a valued resource. *Social Psychology Quarterly, 6,* 1, 103-114.

ICT4D Report. (2009). *Information and Communication Technology for Development.* Cambridge, U.K.: Cambridge University Press.

International Conference on Sustainable Development (2016). Columbia University and The New School New York, September 21-22.

International Monetary Fund (2013). *Concluding statement of the 2013 Article IV Mission to the United States of America. June 14.* Retrievable at http://www.imf.org/external/np/ms/2013/061413.htm.

Irwin, J. R., Slovic, P., Lichtenstein, S. & McClelland, G. (1993). Preference reversals and the measurement of environmental values. *Journal of Risk and Uncertainty, 9,* 5-38.

Janis, I. L. (1982). *Groupthink.* Boston: Houghton Mifflin.

Jervis, R. (1992). Political implications of loss aversion. *Political Psychology, 13,* 2, 187-204.

Kahneman, D., Knetsch, J. L. & Thaler, R. H. (1991). The endowment effect, loss aversion, and status quo bias. *Journal of Economic Perspectives, 5,* 12, 1325-1347.

Kahneman, D. & Ritov, I. (1994). Determinants of stated willingness to pay for public goods: A study in the headline method. *Journal of Risk and Uncertainty, 9,* 5-38.

Kahneman, D. & Tversky, A. (1979). Prospect theory: An analysis of decision under risk. *Econometrica, 47,* 2, 263-292.

Kahneman, D. & Tversky, A. (1992). Advances in prospect theory: Cumulative representation of uncertainty. *Journal of Risk and Uncertainty, 5,* 297-324.

Kahneman, D. & Tversky, A. (2000). *Choices, values, and frames.* Cambridge, U.K.: Cambridge University Press.

Keyes, C. W. (1966). *Cicero, M. T. De republica, De legibus.* The Loeb Classical Library. Cambridge, M.A.: Harvard University Press.

Kirchler, E. (2007). *The economic psychology of tax behaviour.* Cambridge, U.K.: Cambridge University Press.

Koopmans, T. C. (1965). *On the concept of optimal economic growth.* Vatican City: Pontificia Academia Scientarium.

KPMG (2013). *The KPMG Survey of Corporate Responsibility Reporting 2013.* KPMG International.

Laibson, D. (1997). Golden eggs and hyperbolic discounting. *Quarterly Journal of Economics, 112,* 2, 443-447.

Lawson-Remer, T. (2013). Austerity and democracy. *Social Research: An International Quarterly, 80,* 3, 917-928.

Levy, J. S. (1997). Prospect theory, rational choice, and international relations. *International Studies Quarterly, 41,* 1, 87-112.

Loch, C. H., Huberman, B. A. & Stout, S. K. (2000). Status competition and performance in work groups. *Journal of Economic Behavior and Organization, 43,* 35-55.

Loehlin, J. & Nichols, R. (1976). *Heredity, environment and personality.* Austin, T.X.: University of Texas Press.

Loewenstein, G. F., Thompson, L. & Bazerman, M. H. (1989). Social utility and decision-making in interpersonal contexts. *Interpersonal Relations and Group Processes, 57,* 3, 426-441.

Luf, G. (2011). *Grundfragen der Rechtsphilosophie und Rechtsethik: Einführung in die Rechtswissenschaften und ihre Methoden.* Vienna: Manz.

Magdoff, F. & Foster, J. B. (2010). *What every environmentalist needs to know about capitalism: A citizen's guide to capitalism and the environment.* New York, N.Y.: Monthly Review Press.

Mamor, A. (2010). *Philosophy of law.* Princeton, N.J.: Princeton foundations of contemporary philosophy.

Marglin, St. A. & Spiegler, P. (2013). Unpacking the multiplier: Making sense of recent assessment of fiscal stimulus policy. *Social Research: An International Quarterly, 80,* 3, 819-854.

Maslow, A. H. (1943). A theory of human motivation. *Psychological Review, 50,* 370-396.

Matten, D. & Crane, A. (2005). Corporate citizenship: Toward an extended theoretical conceptualization. *Academy of Management Review, 30,* 166-179.

Mayer, H. (2010). *Öffentliches Recht: Einführung in die Rechtswissenschaften und ihre Methoden.* Vienna: Manz.

Mazumder, B. (2008). Earnings mobility in the U.S.: A new look at intergenerational inequality. In S. Bowles, H. Gintis & M. Osborne (Eds.), *Unequal Changes: Family Background and Economic Success,* pp. 145-164, New York, N.Y.: Russell Sage.

Mazur, A. (1973). A cross-species comparison of status in small established groups. *American Sociological Review, 38,* 5, 513-530.

Mazur, A. & Lamb, T. A. (1980). Testosterone, status and mood in human males. *Hormones and Behavior, 14,* 3, 236-246.

McDermott, R., Fowler, J. H. & Smirnov, O. (2008). On the evolutionary origin of prospect theory preferences. *Journal of Politics, 70,* 335-350.

McGahey, R. (2013). The political economy of austerity in the United States. *Social Research: An International Quarterly, 80,* 3, 717-748.

Meeker, B. F. & Weitzel-O'Neill, P. A. (1977). Sex roles and interpersonal behavior in task-oriented groups. *American Sociological Review, 42,* 91-105.

Menchik, P. (1979). Intergenerational transmission of inequality: An empirical study of wealth mobility. *Economica, 46,* 184, 349-362.

Milberg, W. (2013). A note on economic austerity in science, morality, and political economy. *Social Research: An International Quarterly, 80,* 3, 697-714.

Milkman, K. L., Mazza, M. C., Shu, L. L., Tsay, Ch. -J., Bazerman, M. H. (2012). Policy bundling to overcome loss aversion: A method for improving legislative outcomes. *Organizational Behavior and Human Decision Processes,* 117, 158-167.

Moscovici, S. (1961). *La Psychanalyse, son image et son public.* Paris, France: Presses Universitaires de France.

Moscovici, S. (1984). The myth of the lonely paradigm: A rejoinder. *Social Research: An International Quarterly, 51*, 939-968.

Mulligan, C. (1997). *Parental priorities and economic inequality.* Chicago, I.L.: University of Chicago Press.

Nafeez, A. (2013). Pentagon bracing for public dissent over climate and energy shocks: NSA prism is motivated in part by fears that environmentally-linked disasters could spur anti-government activism. *The Guardian*, June 14.

Nisbett, R. & Ross, L. (1980). *Human inference strategies and shortcomings of social judgment.* Englewood Cliffs, N.J.: Prentice Hall.

Nordhaus, W. D. (2008). *A question of balance: Weighting the options on global warming.* New Haven, C.T.: Yale University Press.

Nowak, M. A. & Sigmund, K. (1998). Evolution of indirect reciprocity by image scoring. *Nature, 393*, 573-577.

OECD (2010). *Economic policy reform 2010: Going for growth.* Paris, France: OECD.

OECD (2013). *Education at a glance report.* Paris, France: OECD. Retrievable at http://www.oecd.org/edu/eag2013%20(eng)--FINAL%2020%20June%202013.pdf

Oppenheimer, M., O'Neill, B. C., Webster, M. & Agrawal, S. (2011). Climate change: The limits of consensus. *Science, 317*, 5844, 1505-1506.

Osborne, M. A. (2002). The determinants of individual earnings: Skills, preferences, and schooling. *Journal of Economic Literature, 39*, 4, 1137-1176.

Ostrom, E. (2009). *The Sveriges Riksbank Prize in Economic Sciences in Memory of Alfred Nobel Laureate 2009*, speech.

Panitch, L. & Gindin, S. (2012). *The making of global capitalism: The political economy of American empire.* New York, N.Y.: Verso.

Phelps, E. S. (1961). The golden rule of accumulation: A fable for growthmen. *American Economic Review, 51*, 638-643.

Phelps, E. S. (1966). *Golden roles of economic growth: Studies of efficient and optimal investment.* New York, N.Y.: Norton.

Piketty, T. (2014). *Capital in the 21st century.* Cambridge, M.A.: Harvard University Press.

Piketty, T., Saez, E. & Stantcheva, St. (2011). *Optimal taxation of top labor incomes: A tale of three elasticities.* Center for Economic Policy Research, November, Discussion Paper 8675.

Pollin, R. (2013). Austerity economics and the struggle for the soul of US capitalism. *Social Research: An International Quarterly, 80*, 3, 749-780.

Postlewaite, A. (1998). The social basis of interdependent preferences. *European Economic Review, 42*, 3-5, 779-800.

Proaño, Ch. (2013). On the potential pitfalls of the EU Fiscal Pact: A simulation study of the international dimensions of fiscal austerity. *Social Research: An International Quarterly, 80*, 3, 855-882.

Puaschunder, J. M. (2010). *On corporate and financial social responsibility.* Dissertation University of Vienna.

Puaschunder, J. M. (2015a). *Intergenerational transfer model.* Working paper, New York, N.Y.: The New School for Social Research.

Puaschunder, J. M. (2015b). *Meritocracy and intergenerational mobility.* The Worldly Philosopher Blog. Schwartz Center for Economic Policy Analysis. Retrievable at http://www.economicpolicyresearch.org/index.php/scepa-blog/91-the-worldly-philosopher/1545-meritocracy-builds-equality

Puaschunder, J. M. (2015c). *On eternal equity in the fin-de-millénaire.* Unpublished manuscript. New York, N.Y.: The New School.

Puaschunder, J. M. (2015d). On the social representations of intergenerational equity. *Oxford Journal of Finance and Risk Perspectives, 4,* 4, 78-99.

Puaschunder, J. M. (2015e). *Trust and reciprocity drive social common goods allocation norms.* Proceedings of the Cambridge Business & Economics Conference. Cambridge, U.K.: Cambridge University, Proceedings of the 2015 6th International Conference of the Association of Global Management Studies at Columbia University, New York, N.Y.: The Association of Global Management Studies.

Puaschunder, J. M. (2016a). Intergenerational climate change burden sharing: An economics of climate stability research agenda proposal. *Global Journal of Management and Business Research: Economics and Commerce, 16,* 3, 31-38.

Puaschunder, J. M. (2016b). Putty capital and clay labor: Differing European Union capital and labor freedom speeds in times of European migration. *The New School Economic Review: A Journal of Critical Economics at The New School, 8,* 3, 147-168.

Puaschunder, J. M. (2016c). The beauty of ivy: When inequality meets equality. *Global Journal of Management and Business Research: Economics and Commerce, 16,* 3, 1-11.

Puaschunder, J. M. (2016d). The call for global responsible intergenerational leadership in the corporate world: The quest for an integration of intergenerational equity in contemporary Corporate Social Responsibility (CSR) models. In D. Jamali (Ed.), *Comparative Perspectives in Global Corporate Social Responsibility,* pp. 275-288, Hershey: IGI Global Advances in Business Strategy and Competitive Advantage Book Series.

Puaschunder, J. M. (2017a). *Climate in the 21st century: A macroeconomic model of fair global warming benefits distribution to grant climate justice around the world and over time.* Retrievable at https://papers.ssrn.com/sol3/papers.cfm?abstract_id=2964385

Puaschunder, J. M. (2017b). Cross-sectoral solution-finding and policy dialogue on Information and Communication Technologies for Sustainable Development. In M. Gudic, T. K. Tan & P. M. Flynn (Eds.), *Beyond the Bottom Line: Integrating the UN Global Compact into Management Practices,* pp. 32-46. New York, N.Y.: Greenleaf.

Puaschunder, J. M. (2017c). Ethical decision-making under social uncertainty: An introduction to Überethicality. *Sustainable Production and Consumption, 12,* 78-89.

Puaschunder, J. M. (2017d). *Nudgital: Critique of behavioral political economy.* Retrievable at https://papers.ssrn.com/sol3/papers.cfm?abstract_id=2926276

Puaschunder, J. M. (2017e). The climatorial imperative. *Agriculture Research & Technology, 7*, 4, 1-2.

Puaschunder, J. M. (2017f). *We'll all float on: Global climate change-induced migration and financial flow estimates.* Retrievable at https://papers.ssrn.com/sol3/papers.cfm?abstract_id=2984340

Puaschunder, J. M. (forthcoming a). Mapping climate in the 21st century. *Development.* Palgrave.

Puaschunder, J. M. (forthcoming b). *Governance and climate justice: Global South and developing nations.* Cham: Switzerland: Springer Nature, Palgrave Macmillian: New York, New York.

Puaschunder, J. M. (forthcoming c). *Sunny side up! From climate change burden sharing to fair global warming benefits distribution: Groundwork on the metaphysics of the gains of global warming and the climatorial imperative.* Proceedings of the 2nd Social and Sustainable Finance and Impact Investing Conference, University of Cambridge, September 25, 2017.

Puaschunder, J. M. & Schwarz, G. (2012). *The future is now: How joint decision-making curbs hyperbolic discounting but blurs social responsibility in the intergenerational equity public policy making domain.* Harvard Law School working paper retrievable at http://thesituationist.wordpress.com/2012/12/17/the-situation-of-intergenerational-equity/.

Putnam, R. D. (2015). *Our kids: The American dream in crisis.* New York, N.Y.: Simon & Schuster.

Ramsey, F. P. (1928). A mathematical theory of saving. *Economic Journal, 38,* 152, 543-559.

Rawls, J. (1971). *A theory of justice.* Cambridge, M.A.: Harvard University Press.

Reinfried, Y., Schleicher, A. & Rempfler, A. (2007). Geographical views on education for sustainable development. *Geographiedidaktische Forschungen, 42,* 243-250.

Ridgeway, C. L., Berger, J. & Smith, L. R. (1985). Nonverbal cues and status: An expectation states approach. *American Journal of Sociology, 90,* 5, 955-978.

Ridgeway, C. L. & Walker, H. A. (1995). Status structures. In K. Cook, G. Fine & J. House (Eds.), *Sociological Perspectives on Social Psychology,* pp. 281-310, New York, N.Y.: Allyn & Bacon.

Robson, A. J. (1992). Status, the distribution of wealth, private and social attitudes to risk. *Econometrica, 60,* 4, 837-857.

Roussanov, N. (2009). *Diversification and its discontents: Idiosyncratic and entrepreneurial risk in the quest for social status.* Working paper, Wharton School, University of Pennsylvania.

Sachs, J. D. (2014). Climate change and intergenerational well-being. In L. Bernard & W. Semmler (Eds), *The Oxford Handbook of the Macroeconomics of Global Warming,* pp. 248-259, Oxford, UK.: Oxford University Press.

Samuelson, P. A. (1958). An exact consumption-loan model of interest with or without the social contrivance of money. *Journal of Political Economy, 12,* 467-482.

Samuelson, P. A. (1975a). Optimum social security in a life-cycle growth model. *International Economic Review, 16,* 3, 539-544.

Samuelson, P. A. (1975b). The optimum growth rate for population. *International Economic Review, 16*, 3, 531-538.

Savin-Williams, R. C. (1979). Dominance hierarchies in groups of early adolescents. *Child Development, 50*, 4, 923-935.

Schkade, D. A. & Kahneman, D. (1998). Does living in California make people happy? A focusing illusion in judgments of life satisfaction. *Psychological Science, 9*, 5, 340-346.

Semmler, W. (2013). The macroeconomics of austerity in the European Union. *Social Research: An International Quarterly, 80*, 3, 883-914.

Semmler, W., Greiner, A., Diallo, B., Rajaram, A. & Rezai, A. (2011). Fiscal policy, public expenditures composition and growth: Theory and empirics. *The IEB International Journal of Finance, 2*, 1-42.

Shaikh, A. (2013). Crisis, austerity, and the role of economic theory in policy. *Social Research: An International Quarterly, 80*, 3, 653-664.

Shell, K. (1967). *Essays on the theory of optimal growth.* Cambridge, M.A.: MIT Press.

Sidanius, J. & Pratto, F. (1999). *Social dominance: An intergroup theory of social hierarchy and oppression.* New York, N.Y.: Cambridge University Press.

Siegel, J. J. (2002). *Stocks for the long run.* New York, N.Y.: McGraw Hill.

Slaper, T. F. and Hall, T. J. (2011) *The triple bottom line: What is it and how does it work?*
http://www.ibrc.indiana.edu/ibr/2011/spring/article2.html

Slawinski, N. & Bansal, P. (2012). A matter of time: The temporal perspectives of organizational responses to climate change. *Organization Studies, 33*, 11, 1537-1563.

Solon, G. R. (1992). Intergenerational income mobility in the United States. *American Economic Review, 82*, 3, 393-408.

Solon, G. R. (1999). Intergenerational mobility in the labor market. In O. Ashenfelter & D. Card (Eds.), *Handbook of Labor Economics*, pp. 1761-1800, New Holland: Elsevier.

Solow, R. (1956). A contribution to the theory of economic growth. *Quarterly Journal of Economics, 70*, 65-94.

Stein, J. (2011). *The diversity of debt crises in Europe.* CESIFO Working Paper No. 3348, Category 6: Fiscal Policy, Macroeconomics and Growth, February.

Stern, N. (2006). Stern review: The economics of climate change. Retrievable at
http://www.brown.edu/Departments/Economics/Faculty/Matthew_Turner/ec1340/readings/Sternreview_full.pdf

Steurer, R., Martinuzzi, R.-A. & Margula, S. (2012). Public policies on CSR in Europe: Themes, instruments and regional differences. *Corporate Social Responsibility and Environmental Management, 19*, 206-227.

Stiglitz, J. (1998). The private uses of public interests: Incentives and institutions. *Journal of Economic Perspectives, 12*, 3-22.

Streeck, W. (2011). *The crisis in context: Democratic capitalism and its contradictions.* MPIfG Working Paper. Cologne: Max Planck Institute for the Study of Societies.

Sustainable Development Goals Report: The People's Agenda (2016). UNA-UK.

Swan, T. W. (1964). Growth models: Of golden ages and production functions. In K. Berrill (Ed.), *Economic Development for Asia*, pp. 3-16, London, U.K.: Macmillan.

Taubman, P. (1976). The determinants of earnings: Genetic, family, and other environments: A study of white male twins. *American Economic Review, 66*, 5, 858-870.

Tajfel, H. (1978). *Differentiation between social groups: Studies in the social psychology of intergroup relations.* London, U.K.: Academic Press.

Tajfel, H. & Turner, J. C. (1979). An integrative theory of intergroup conflict. In W. G. Austin & St. Worchel (Eds.), *The Social Psychology of Intergroup Relations, pp. 94-109, Monterey: Brooks-Cole.*

Tajfel, H. & Turner, J. C. (1986). The social identity theory of inter-group behavior. In S. Worchel & L. W. Austin (Eds.), *Psychology of Intergroup Relations*, pp. 7-24, Chicago, I.L.: Nelson-Hall.

Tenbrunsel, A. E. & Messick, D. M. (2004). Ethical fading: The role of self-deception in unethical behavior. *Social Justice Research, 17*, 2, 223-236.

Thaler, R. H. (1999). Mental accounting matters. *Journal of Behavioral Decision-making, 12*, 183-206.

Thaler, R. H. & Sunstein, C. S. (2008). *Nudge: Improving decision-making about health, wealth and happiness.* New Haven, C.T.: Yale University Press.

Tiedens, L. Z. (2000). Powerful emotions: The vicious cycle of social status positions and emotions. In N. M. Ashkanasy & C. E. Haertel (Eds.), *Emotions in the Workplace: Research, Theory, and Practice*, pp. 72-81, Westport: Greenwood.

Tobin, J. (1967). Life cycle saving and balanced growth. In I. Fisher & W. Fellner (Eds.), *Ten Economic Studies in the Tradition of Irving Fisher*, pp. 231-256, New York, N.Y.: Wiley.

Tooby, J. & Cosmides, L. (1990). The past explains the present: Emotional adaptations and the structure of ancestral environments. *Ethology and Sociobiology, 11*, 375-424.

Tversky, A. & Kahneman, D. (1974). Judgment under uncertainty: Heuristics and biases. *Science, 185*, 1124-1131.

Tversky, A. & Kahneman, D. (1991). Loss aversion in riskless choice: A reference dependent model. *Quarterly Journal of Economics, 41*, 1039-1041.

Tversky, A. & Shafir, E. (1992). Choice under conflict: The dynamics of deferred decision. *Psychological Science, 3*, 6, 358-361.

Tyler, T. R. (1990). *Why people obey the law: Procedural justice, legitimacy, and compliance.* New Haven, C.T.: Yale University Press.

Veerle, M. (2011). *Cooking, caring and volunteering: Unpaid work around the world.* Paris, France: OECD Social, employment and migration working paper 116.

Volscho, Th. W. & Kelly, N. J. (2012). The rise of the super-rich: Power resources, taxes, financial markets, and the dynamics of the top 1 percent, 1949 to 2008. *American Sociological Review, 77*, 5, 679-699.

von Weizsäcker, C. Ch. (1962). *Wachstum, Zins, und optimale Investitionsquote.* Basel: Kyklos.

Wade-Benzoni, K. A. & Tost, L. P. (2009). The egoism and altruism of intergenerational behavior. *Personality and Social Psychology Review, 13,* 165-193.

Washington Post (2013). *We still need a grand bargain,* June 9.

Weber, M. (1946/2009). *Essays in sociology.* Oxford, UK.: Oxford University Press.

Weber, M. (1978). *Economy and society.* Berkeley, C.A.: University of California Press.

Wedekind, C. (1998). Enhanced: Give and ye shall be recognized. *Science, 280,* 2070-2071.

Weisband, S. P., Schneider, S. K. & Connolly, T. (1995). Computer-mediated communication and social information: Status salience and status differences. *Academy of Management Journal, 38,* 4, 1124-1151.

World Development Report: Mind, society, and behavior (2015). Washington, D.C.: World Bank.

World Economic Forum 2015 Report. Davos, Switzerland: World Economic Forum.

Young, I. M. (2011). *Responsibility for justice.* Oxford, UK.: Oxford University Press.

Zaretsky, E. (2015). Lecture notes. GECO 5250: *Rethinking capitalism.* Spring 2015. New York, N.Y.: The New School.

Zimbardo, Ph. (2011a). *My journey from evil to heroism.* Speech delivered at Webster University. May 31, 2011. Vienna, Austria, EU.

Zimbardo, Ph. (2011b). *Evil no! Heroes yes!* Speech delivered at Harvard Law School. October 26, 2011. Cambridge, M.A., USA.

Index

A

B

C

D

E

H

I

J

K

O

P

R

S

T

U

V

W

Y